I0748996

Mrs L. W. Felch

Ann Arbor

Dec 1861.

TIMOTHY TITCOMB'S WORKS.

I.—LETTERS TO YOUNG PEOPLE; SINGLE AND MARRIED. (26th Edition.) One vol. 12mo. $1 00; gilt edges, $1 50.

II.—BITTER-SWEET; A POEM. (15th Edition.) One vol. 12mo. $0 75; gilt edges, $1 25.

III.—GOLD-FOIL; HAMMERED FROM POPULAR PROVERBS. (15th Edition.) One vol. 12mo. $1 00; gilt edges, $1 50.

IV.—MISS GILBERT'S CAREER; AN AMERICAN STORY. (13th Edition.) One vol. 12mo. $1 25.

V.—LESSONS IN LIFE. A SERIES OF FAMILIAR ESSAYS. One vol. 12mo. $1 00; gilt edges, $1 50.

☞ Copies sent by mail, post-paid, on receipt of price.

LESSONS IN LIFE.

A

SERIES OF FAMILIAR ESSAYS.

BY

TIMOTHY TITCOMB,

AUTHOR OF "LETTERS TO THE YOUNG," "GOLD-FOIL," ETC.

NEW YORK:
CHARLES SCRIBNER, 124 GRAND STREET.
1861.

Entered, according to Act of Congress, in the year 1861,
By CHARLES SCRIBNER,
In the Clerk's Office of the District Court of the United States for the Southern District of New York.

JOHN F. TROW,
PRINTER, STEREOTYPER, AND ELECTROTYPER,
48 & 50 Greene Street,
New York.

PREFACE.

THE quick and cordial reception which greeted the author's "Letters to the Young," and his more recent series of essays entitled "Gold Foil," and the constant and substantial friendship which has been maintained by the public toward those productions, must stand as his apology for this third venture in a kindred field of effort. It should be —and probably is—unnecessary for the author to say that in this book, as in its predecessors, he has aimed to be neither brilliant nor profound. He has endeavored, simply, to treat in a familiar and attractive way a few of the more prominent questions which concern the life of every thoughtful man and woman. Indeed, he can hardly pretend to have done more than to organize, and put into form, the average thinking of those who read his books—to place before the people the sum of their own choicer judgments—and he neither expects nor wishes for these essays higher praise than that which accords to them the quality of common sense.

SPRINGFIELD, MASS.,
November, 1861.

CONTENTS.

LESSONS IN LIFE.

LESSON I.

MOODS AND FRAMES OF MIND.

"That blessed mood
In which the burden of the mystery,
In which the heavy and the weary weight
Of all this unintelligible world
Is lightened." WORDSWORTH.

"Oh, blessed temper, whose unclouded ray
Can make to-morrow cheerful as to-day."
POPE.

"My heart and mind and self, never in tune;
Sad for the most part, then in such a flow
Of spirits, I seem now hero, now buffoon."
LEIGH HUNT.

IT rained yesterday; and, though it is midsummer, it is unpleasantly cool to-day. The sky is clear, with almost a steel-blue tint, and the meadows are very deeply green. The shadows among the woods are black and massive, and the whole face of nature looks painfully clean, like that of a healthy little boy who has been bathed in a chilly room with very cold water. I notice that I am sensitive to a change like this, and that my mind goes very reluctantly to its task this morning. I look out from my window, and think how delightful it would be to take a seat in the sun, down under the fence, across the street. It seems to me that if I could sit there awhile, and get warm, I could think better and write better. Toasting in the sunlight is conducive rather to reverie than thought, or I should be inclined to try it. This reluctance to commence labor, and this looking out of the window and longing for an accession of strength, or warmth, or inspiration, or something or other not easily named, calls back to me an experience of childhood.

It was summer, and I was attending school. The seats were hard, and the lessons were dry, and the walls of the school-room were very cheerless. An indulgent, sweet-faced girl was my teacher; and I presume that she felt the irksomeness of the confinement quite as severely as I did. The weather was delightful, and the birds were singing everywhere; and the thought came to me, that if I could only stay out of doors, and lie down in the shadow of a tree, I could get my lesson. I begged the privilege of trying the experiment. The kind heart that presided over the school-room could not resist my petition; so I was soon lying in the coveted shadow. I went to work very severely; but the next moment found my eyes wandering; and heart, feeling, and fancy were going up and down the earth in the most vagrant fashion. It was hopeless dissipation to sit under the tree; and discovering a huge rock on the hillside, I made my way to that, to try what virtue there might be in a shadow not produced by foliage. Seated under the brow of the boulder, I again applied myself to the dim-looking text, but it had become utterly meaningless; and a musical cricket under the rock would have put me to sleep if I had permitted myself to remain. I found that neither tree nor rock would lend me help; but down in the meadow I saw the brook sparkling, and spanning it, a little bridge where I had been accustomed to sit, hanging my feet over the water, and angling for minnows. It seemed as if the bridge and the water might do something for me, and, in a few minutes, my feet were dangling from the accustomed seat. There, almost under my nose, close to the bottom of the clear, cool stream, lay a huge speckled trout, fanning the sand with his slow fins, and minding nothing about me at all. What could a boy do with Colburn's First Lessons, when a living trout, as large and nearly as long as his arm, lay almost within the reach of his fingers? How long I sat there I do not know, but the tinkle of a distant bell startled me, and I startled the trout, and fish and vision faded before the terrible consciousness that I knew less of my lesson than I did when I left the school-house.

This has always been my fortune when running after, or looking for, moods. There is a popular hallucination that makes of authors a romantic people who are entirely dependent upon moods and moments of inspiration for the power to labor in their peculiar way. Authors are supposed to write when they "feel like it," and at no other time. Visions of Byron with a gin-bottle at his side, and a beautiful woman hanging over his shoulder, dashing off a dozen stanzas of Childe Harold at a sitting, flit through the brains of sentimental youth. We hear of women who are seized suddenly by an idea, as if it were a colic, or a flea, often at midnight, and are obliged to rise and dispose of it in some way. We are told of very delicate girls who carry pencils and cards with them, to take the names and address of such angels as may visit them in out-of-the-way places. We read of poets who go on long sprees, and after recovery retire to their rooms and work night and day, eating not and sleeping little, and in some miraculous way producing wonderful literary creations. The mind of a literary man is supposed to be like a shallow summer brook, that turns a mill. There is no water except when it rains, and the weather being very fickle, it is never known when there will be water. Sometimes, however, there comes a freshet, and then the mill runs night and day, until the water subsides, and another dry time comes on.

Now, while I am aware, as every writer must be, that the brain works very much better at some times than it does at others, I can declare without reservation, that no man who depends upon moods for the power to write can possibly accomplish much. I know men who rely upon their moods, alike for the disposition and the ability to write, but they are, without exception, lazy and inefficient men. They never have accomplished much, and they never will accomplish much. Regular eating, regular sleeping, regular working—these are the secrets of all true literary success. A man may throw off a single little poem by a spasm, but he cannot write a poem of three thousand lines by spasms. Spasms that produce poems like this, must last from five to seven hours a day, through six days of every week, and four weeks of every month, until the work shall be finished. There is no good reason why the mind will not do its best by regular exercise and usage. The mower starts in the morning with a lame back and with aching joints; but he keeps on mowing, and the glow rises, and the perspiration starts, and he becomes interested in his labor, and, at length, he finds himself at work with full efficiency. He was not in the mood for mowing when he began, but mowing brought its own mood, and he knew it would when he began. The mind is sometimes lame in the morning. It refuses to go to work. Our wills seem entirely insufficient to drive it to its tasks; but if it be driven to its work and held to it persistently, and held thus every day, it will ultimately be able to do its best every day. A man who works his brains for a living, must work them just as regularly as the omnibus-driver does his horses.

We sometimes go to church and hear a preacher who depends upon his moods for the power to preach his best. He preaches well, and we say that he is in the mood; and then again he preaches poorly, and we say that he is not in the mood. A public singer who has the power to move us at her will, comes into the concert-room, and gives her music without spirit and without making any apparent effort to please. We say that Madame or Mademoiselle is "not in the mood to-night." A lecturer has his moods, which, apparently, he slips on and off as he would a dressing-gown, charming the people of one town by his eloquence and elegance, and disgusting another by his dullness and carelessness. We are in the habit of saying that certain men are very unequal in their performances, which is only a way of saying that they are moody, and dependent upon and controlled by moods. I think that, in any work or walk of life, a man can in a great degree become the master of his moods, so that, as a preacher, or a singer, or a lecturer, he can do his best every time quite as regularly as a writer can do his best every time. Mr. Benedict somewhat inelegantly remarked, when in this country, that the reason of Jenny Lind's success was, that she "made a conscience of her art." If we had asked Mr. Benedict to explain himself, he probably would have said that she conscientiously did her best every time, in every place. This was true of Jenny Lind. She never failed. She sang just as well in the old church where the country people had flocked to greet her, as in the halls of the metropolis. Yet Jenny Lind was decidedly a woman of moods, and indulged in them when she could afford it.

The power of the will over moods of the mind is very noticeable in children. Children often rise in the morning in any thing but an amiable frame of mind. Petulant, impatient, quarrelsome, they cannot be spoken to or touched without producing an explosion of ill-nature. Sleep seems to have been a bath of vinegar to them, and one would think the fluid had invaded their mouth and nose, and eyes and ears, and had been absorbed by every pore of their sensitive skins. In a condition like this, I have seen them bent over the parental knee, and their persons subjected to blows from the parental palm; and they have emerged from the infliction with the vinegar all expelled, and their faces shining like the morning—the transition complete and satisfactory to all the parties. Three-quarters of the moods that men and women find themselves in, are just as much under the control of the will as this. The man who rises in the morning, with his feelings all bristling like the quills of a hedge-hog, simply needs to be knocked down. Like a solution of certain salts, he requires a rap to make him crystallize. A great many mean things are done in the family for which moods are put forward as the excuse, when the moods themselves are the most inexcusable things of all. A man or a woman in tolerable health has no moral right to indulge in an unpleasant mood, or to depend upon moods for the performance of the duties of life. If a bad mood come to such persons as these, it is to be shaken off by a direct effort of the will, under all circumstances.

There are moods, however, for which men are not responsible, and the parent of these is sickness—the feeble or inharmonious movements of the body. When my little boy wakes in the morning, his smile is as bright as the pencil of sunlight that lies across his coverlet; but when evening comes, he is peevish and fretful. The little limbs are weary, and the mood is produced by weariness. So my friend with a harassing cough is in a melancholy mood, and my bilious friend is in a severe and savage mood, or in a dark and gloomy mood, or in a petulant mood, or in a fearful or foreboding mood. In truth, bile is the prolific mother of moods. The stream of life flows through the biliary duct. When that is obstructed, life is obstructed. When the golden tide sets back upon the liver, it is like back-water under a mill; it stops the driving-wheel. Bile spoils the peace of families, breaks off friendships, cuts off man from communion with his Maker, colors whole systems of theology, transforms brains into putty, and destroys the comfort of a jaundiced world. The famous Dr. Abernethy had his hobby, as most famous men have; and this hobby was "blue pill and ipecac," which he prescribed for every thing, with the supposition, I presume, that all disease has its origin in the liver. Most moods, I am sure, have their birth in the derangements of this important organ; and while the majority of them can be controlled, there are others for which their victims are not responsible. There are men who cannot insult me, because I will not take an insult from them any more than I would from a man intoxicated. When their bile starts, I am sure they will come to me and apologize.

We all have acquaintances who are men of moods. Whenever we meet them, we try to determine which of their moods is dominant, that we may know how to treat them. If the severe mood be on, we would just as soon think of whistling at a funeral as indulging in a jest; but if the cloud be off, we have a sprightly friend and a pleasant time with him. Goldsmith's pedagogue was a man of moods, and his pupils understood them.

"A man severe he was, and stern to view;
I knew him well, and every truant knew:
Well had the boding tremblers learned to trace
The day's disasters in his morning face;
Full well they laughed with counterfeited glee
At all his jokes, for many a joke had he;
Full well the busy whisper, circling round,
Conveyed the dismal tidings when he frowned."

While I maintain that a man can generally be the master of his moods, I am very well aware that but few men are; and it is wise for us to know how to deal with them. The secret of many a man's success in the world resides in his insight into the moods of men, and his tact in dealing with them. Modern Christian philanthropists tell us that if we would do good to the soul of a starving child, we must first put food into his mouth, and comfortable clothing upon his body. This, by way of manifesting a practical interest in his welfare, and paving our way to his heart by a form of kindness which he can thoroughly appreciate. But there is more in such an act than this,—we change his mood. From a mood of despair or discouragement, we translate him into a mood of cheerfulness and hopefulness; and then we have a soul to deal with that is surrounded by the conditions of improvement. There is much more than divine duty and Christian forgiveness in the injunction: "if thine enemy hunger, feed him; if he thirst, give him drink." The highest wisdom would dictate such a policy for changing his mood, and bringing him into a condition in which he could entertain a sense of his meanness.

It is curious to see how much fulness and emptiness of stomach have to do with moods. A business man who has been at work hard all day, will enter his house for dinner as crabbed as a hungry bear—crabbed because he is as hungry as a hungry bear. The wife understands the mood, and, while she says little to him, is careful not to have the dinner delayed. In the mean time, the children watch him cautiously, and do not tease him with questions. When the soup is gulped, and he leans back and wipes his mouth, there is an evident relaxation, and his wife ventures to ask for the news. When the roast beef is disposed of, she presumes upon gossip, and possibly upon a jest; and when, at last, the dessert is spread upon the table, all hands are merry, and the face of the husband and father, which entered the house so pinched and savage and sharp, becomes soft and full and beaming as the face of the round summer moon. Children are very sensitive to the influence of hunger; and often when we think that we are witnessing some fearful proof of the total depravity of human nature in a young child, we are only witnessing the natural expression of a desire for bread and milk. The politicians and all that class of men who have axes to grind, understand this business very thoroughly. If a measure is to be carried through, and any man wishes to secure votes for it, he gives a dinner. If a man wishes for a profitable contract, he gives a dinner. If he is up for a fat office, he gives a dinner. If it is desirable that a pair of estranged friends be brought together, and reconciled to each other, they are invited to a dinner. If hostile interests are to be harmonized, and clashing measures compromised, and divergent forces brought into parallelism, all must be effected by means of a dinner. A good dinner produces a good mood,—at least, it produces an impressible mood. The will relaxes wonderfully under the influence of iced champagne, and canvas-backs are remarkable softeners of prejudice. The daughter of Herodias took Herod at a great disadvantage, when she came in and danced before him and his friends at his birth-day supper, and secured the head of John the Baptist. No one, I presume, believes that if she had undertaken to dance before him when he was hungry, she would have had the offer of a gift equal to the half of his kingdom. It is more than likely that, under any other circumstances, she would have been told to "sit down and show less." It is by means of food and drink, and various entertainments of the senses, that moods are manufactured, and used as media of approach to the wills which it is desirable to bend or direct.

I have found moods to be very poor tests of character. Having cut through the crust of a most forbidding mood, produced by bodily derangement or constant and pressing labor of the brain, I have often found a heart full of all the sweetest and richest traits of humanity. I have found, too, that some natures know the door that leads through the moods of other natures. There are men who never present their moody side to me. My neighbor enters their presence and finds them severe in aspect, hard in feeling, and abrupt in speech. I go in immediately after, and open the door right through that mood, into the genial good heart that sits behind it, and the door always flies open when I come. I know men whose mood is usually exceedingly pleasant. There is a glow of health upon their faces. Their words are musical to women and children. They are cheerful and chipper and sunshiny, and not easily moved to anger; and yet I know them to be liars and full of selfishness. Under their sweet mood, which sound health and a not over-sensitive conscience and the satisfactions of sense engender, they conceal hearts that are as false and foul as any that illustrate the reign of sin in human nature. Many a Christian has times of feeling that God is in a special manner smiling upon him, and communing with him, and filling him with the peace and joy that only flow from heavenly fountains, when the truth is that he is only in a good mood. He is well, all the machinery of his mind and body is playing harmoniously, and, of course, he feels well, and that is all there is about it. He is not a better Christian than he was when he slipped into the mood, and no better than he will be when he slips out of it. If he really be a good Christian, his moods operate like clouds and blue sky. The sun shines all the time, and the cloudy moods only hide it;—they do not extinguish it.

There are many sad cases of insanity of a religious character which originate in moods. A man, through a period of health, has a bright and cheerful religious experience. The world looks pleasant to him, the heavens smile kindly upon him, and the Divine Spirit witnesses with his own that he is at peace and in harmony with God. Joy thrills him as he greets the morning light, and peace nestles upon his heart as he lies down to his nightly rest. He feels in his soul the influx of spiritual life from the Great Source of all life, as he opens it in worship and in prayer. But at length there comes a change. A strange sadness creeps into his heart. The sky that was once so bright has become dark. The prayer that once rose as easily as incense upon the still morning air, straight toward heaven, will not rise at all, but settles like smoke upon him, and fills his eyes with tears. Something seems to have come between him and his God. Strange, accusing voices are heard within him. However deep the agony that moves him, he cannot rend the cloud that interposes between him and his Maker. This, now, is simply a mood produced by ill health; and I hope that everybody who reads this will remember it. Remember that God never changes, that a man's moods are constantly changing, and that when a man earnestly seeks for spiritual peace, and cannot find it, and thinks that he has committed the unpardonable sin without knowing it, he is bilious, and needs medical treatment. Alas! what multitudes of sad souls have walked out of this hopeless mood into a life-long insanity, when all they needed in the first place, perhaps, was a dose of blue pills, or half a dozen strings of tenpins, or a sea-voyage sufficiently rough for "practical purposes."

This subject I find to be abundantly prolific, and I see that I have been able to do hardly more than to hint at its more prominent aspects. It seems to me that moods only need to be studied more, and to be better understood, to bring them very much under the domain of our wills. A great deal is learned when we know what a mood is, and know that we are subject to varying frames of mind, resulting from causes which affect our health. If I know that I am impatient and cross because I am hungry, then I know how to get rid of my mood, and how to manage it until I do get rid of it. If I feel unable to labor, not because I am feeble, but because I am not in the mood, then I have the mood in my hands, to be dealt with intelligently. If my reason tell me that it is only a mood that hides from me the face of my Maker, my reason will also tell me that my first business is to get rid of my mood, and that my will must approach the work, directly or indirectly. We are always and necessarily in some mood of mind—in some condition of passion or feeling. It is the intensification and the dominant influence of moods that are to be guarded against or destroyed. Moods are dangerous only when they obscure reason, and destroy self-control, and disturb the mental poise, and become the media of false impressions from all the life around us and within us.

LESSON II.

BODILY IMPERFECTIONS AND IMPEDIMENTS.

"I that am curtailed of this fair proportion,
Cheated of feature by dissembling nature,
Deformed, unfinished, sent before my time
Into this breathing world, scarce half made up."
RICHARD III.

"None can be called deformed but the unkind."
SHAKSPEARE.

"'Tis true, his nature may with faults abound;
But who will cavil when the heart is sound?"
STEPHEN MONTAGUE.

IT is a bright June morning. The fresh grass is loaded with dew, every bead of which sparkles in the light of the brilliant sun. A big, yellow-shouldered bee comes booming through the open window, and buzzes up and down my room, and threatens my shrinking ears, and then dives through the window again; and his form recedes and his hum dies away, as if it were the note of a reed-stop in the "swell" of a church organ. There is such confusion in the songs of the birds, that I can hardly select the different notes, so as to name their owners. There is a great deal of bird-singing that is simply what a weaver would call "filling." Robins and bobolinks and blue-birds and sundry other favorites furnish the warp, and color and characterize the tapestry of a flowing, vocal morning; while the little, gray-backed multitude work in the neutral ground tones, and bring the sweeter and more elaborate notes into beautiful relief. Thus, with a little aid of imagination, I get up some very exquisite fabrics—vocal silks and satins:—robins on a field of chickadees; bobolinks and thrushes alternately on a hit-or-miss ground of blackbirds, wrens, and pewees. Into the midst of all this delicious confusion there breaks a note that belongs to another race of creatures; and as I look from my window, and see the singer, my eyes fill with tears. It is a little boy, possibly twelve years old, though he looks younger, walking with a crutch. One withered limb dangles as he goes. He is a cripple for life; yet his face is as bright and cheerful as the face of the morning itself; and what do you think he is singing? "Hail Columbia, happy land," at the top of his lungs! The birds are merrily wheeling over his head, and diving through the air, and moving here and there as freely as the wind, yet not one among them carries a lighter heart than that which he is jerking along by the side of the little crutch.

As I see how cheerfully he bears the burden of his hopeless halting, there comes back to me the story of the lame lord who sang a different sort of song—the lame lord who died at Missolonghi, and whose friend Trelawny—human jackal that he was—stole to his bedside after the breath had left his body, and examined his clubbed feet, and then went away and wrote about them. Here was a man with regal gifts of mind—a poet of splendid genius—a titled aristocrat—a man admired and praised wherever the English language was read—a man who knew that he held within himself the power to make his name immortal—a man with wealth sufficient for all grateful luxuries—yet with clubbed feet; and those feet! Ah! how they embittered and spoiled that man of magnificent achievements and sublime possibilities! It would appear, from the disgusting narrative of Mr. Trelawny, that he was in reality the only man who had ever seen Byron's feet. Those feet had been kept so closely hidden, or so cunningly disguised, that nobody had known their real deformity; and the poor lord who had carried them through his thirty-six years of life, had done it in constantly tormented and mortified pride. Those misshapen organs had an important agency in making him a misanthropic, morbidly sensitive, unhappy, desperate man. When he sang, he did not forget them; and the poor fools who turned down their shirt-collars, and imitated his songs, and thought they were inspired by his winged genius, had under them only a pair of halting, clubbed feet.

There is a class of unfortunate men and women in the world to whom the boy and the bard have introduced us. They are not all lame: but they all think they have cause to be dissatisfied with the bodies God has given them. Perhaps they are simply ugly, and are aware that no one can look in their faces with other thought than that they are ugly. Now it is a pleasant thing to have a pleasant face, and an agreeable form. It is pleasant for a man to be large, well-shaped, and good-looking, and it is unpleasant for him to be small, and to carry an ill-shaped form and an ugly face. It is pleasant for a woman to feel that she has personal attractions for those around her, and it is unpleasant for her to feel that no man can ever turn his eyes admiringly upon her. A misshapen limb, a hump in the back, a withered arm, a shortened leg, a clubbed foot, a hare-lip, an unwieldy corpulence, a hideous leanness, a bald head—all these are unpleasant possessions, and all these, I suppose, give their possessors, first and last, a great deal of pain. Then there is the taint of an unpopular blood, that a whole race carry with them as a badge of humiliation. I have heard of Africans who declared that they would willingly go through the pain of being skinned alive, if, at the close of the operation, they could become white men. There are men of genius, with plenty of white blood in their veins—with only a trace of Africa in their faces—whose lives are embittered by that trace; and who know that the pure Anglo Saxon, if he follows his instincts, will say to him: "Thus far,"—(through a limited range of relations.)—"but no further."

From the depths of my soul I pity a man or woman who bears about an irremediable bodily deformity, or the mark of the blood of a humiliated race. I pity any human being who carries around a body that he feels to be in any sense an unpleasant one to those whom he meets. I pity the deformed man, and the maimed man, and the terribly ugly man, and the black man, and the white man with black blood in him, because he usually feels that these things bear with them a certain degree of humiliation. I pity the man who is not able to stand out in the broad sunlight, with other men, and to feel that he has as goodly a frame and as fine blood and as pleasant a presence as the average of those he sees around him. I do not wonder at all that many of these persons become soured and embittered and jealous. A sensitive mind, dwelling long upon misfortunes of this peculiar character, will inevitably become morbid; and multitudes of humbler men than Lord Byron have cursed their fate as bitterly as he, and have even lifted their eyes to blaspheme the Being who made them.

The two instances which I have mentioned show us that there are two ways of taking misfortunes of this character; and one of them seems to a good deal better than the other. Between the boy who ignored the withered leg and the crutch, and the proud poet who permitted a slight personal deformity to darken his whole life, there is a distance like that between heaven and earth.

I believe in the law of compensation. Human lot is, on the whole, well averaged. A man does not possess great gifts of person and of mind without drawbacks somewhere. Either great duties are imposed upon him, or great burdens are put upon his shoulders, or great temptations assail and harass him. Something in his life, at some time in his life, takes it upon itself to reduce his advantages to the average standard. Nature gave Byron clubbed feet, but with those feet she gave him a genius whose numbers charmed the world —a genius which multitudes of commonplace or weak men would have been glad to purchase at the price of almost any humiliating eccentricity of person. But they were obliged to content themselves with excellent feet, and brains of the common kind and calibre. Providence had withered the little boy's leg, but the loudest song I have heard from a boy in a twelvemonth came from his lips, as he limped along alone in the open street. The cheerful heart in his bosom was a great compensation for the withered leg; and beyond this the boy had reason for singing over the fact that he was forever released from military duty, and firemen's duty, and all racing about in the service of other people. There are individual cases of misfortune in which it is hard to detect the compensating good, but these we must call the "exceptions" which "prove the rule."

But the best of all compensation for natural defects and deformities, is that which comes in the form of a peculiar love. The mother of a poor, misshapen, idiotic boy, will, though she have half a score of bright and beautiful children besides, entertain for him a peculiar affection. He may not be able, in his feeble-mindedness, to appreciate it, but her heart brims with tenderness for him. The delicate morsel is reserved for him; and, if he be a sufferer, the softest pillow and the tenderest nursing will be his. A love will be bestowed upon him which gold could not buy, and which no beauty of person and no brilliancy of natural gifts could possibly awaken. It is thus with every case of defect or eccentricity of person. So sure as the mother of a child sees in that child's person any reason for the world to regard it with contempt or aversion, does she treat it with peculiar tenderness; as if she were commissioned by God—as indeed she is—to make up to it in the best coinage that which the world will certainly neglect to bestow.

With the world at large, however, there are certain conditions on which this variety of compensation is rendered; and a man who would have compensation for defects of person, must accept these conditions, or furnish them. Such a man as Lord Byron would have been offended by pity. To have been commiserated on his misfortune, would have made him exceedingly angry. He would not allow himself to be treated as an unfortunate man. He bound up his feet, and made efforts to walk that ended in intense pain, rather than appear the lame man that he really was. Of course, there was no compensation in the tender pity and affectionate consideration of the world for him; nor is there any for the sad unfortunates who inherit and exercise his spirit. But for all those who accept their life with all its conditions, in a cheerful spirit, who give up their pride, who take their bodies as God formed them, and make the best of them, there is abundant compensation in the affection of the world. A cheerful spirit, exercised in weakness, infirmity, calamity—any sort of misfortune—is just as sure to awaken a peculiarly affectionate interest in all observers, as a lighted lamp is to illuminate the objects around it. I know of men and women who are the favorites of a whole neighborhood—nay, a whole town—because they are cheerful, and courageous, and self-respectful under misfortune; and I know of those who are as much dreaded as a pestilence, because they will not accept their lot—because they grow bitter and jealous—and because they will persist in taunts and complaints.

The number of those who are, or who consider themselves, unfortunate in their physical conformation, is larger than the most of us suppose. I presume that at least one-half of the readers of this essay are any thing but well satisfied with the "tabernacle" in which they reside. One man wishes he were a little larger; one woman wishes she were a little smaller; one does not like her complexion, or the color of her eyes and hair; one has a nose too large; another has a nose too small; one has round shoulders; another has a low forehead; and so every one becomes a critic of his or her style of structure. When we find a man or a woman who is absolutely faultless in form and features, we usually find a fool. I do not remember that I ever met a very handsome man or woman, who was not as vain and shallow as a peacock. I recently met a magnificent woman of middle age at a railroad station. She was surrounded by all those indescribable somethings and nothings which mark the rich and well-bred traveller, and her face was queenly—not sweet and pretty like a doll's face—but handsome and stylish, and strikingly impressive, so that no man could look at her once without turning to look again; yet I had not been in her presence a minute, before I found, to my utter disgust, that the old creature was as vain of her charms as a spoiled girl, and gloried in the attention which she was conscious her face everywhere attracted. It would seem as if nature, in making up mankind, had always been a little short of materials, so that, if special attention were bestowed upon the form and face, the brain suffered; and if the brain received particular attention, why then there was something lacking in the body.

This large class of malcontents generally find some way of convincing themselves, however, that they are as good-looking as the average of mankind. They make a good deal of some special points of beauty, and imagine that these quite overshadow their defects. Still, there is a portion of them who can never do this; and I think of them with a sadness which it is impossible for me to express. For a homely—even an ugly man—I have no pity to spare. I never saw one so ugly yet, that if he had brains and a heart, he could not find a beautiful woman sensible enough to marry him. But for the hopelessly plain and homely sisters—"these tears!" There is a class of women who know that they possess in their persons no attractions for men,—that their faces are homely, that their frames are ill-formed, that their carriage is clumsy, and that, whatever may be their gifts of mind, no man can have the slightest desire to possess their persons. That there are compensations for these women, I have no doubt, but many of them fail to find them. Many of them feel that the sweetest sympathies of life must be repressed, and that there is a world of affection from which they must remain shut out forever. It is hard for a woman to feel that her person is not pleasing—harder than for a man to feel thus. I would tell why, if it were necessary—for there is a bundle of very interesting philosophy tied up in the matter—but I will content myself with stating the fact, and permitting my readers to reason about it as they will.

Now, if a homely woman, soured and discouraged by her lot, becomes misanthropic and complaining, she will be as little loved as she is admired; but if she accepts her lot good-naturedly, makes up her mind to be happy, and is determined to be agreeable in all her relations to society, she will be everywhere surrounded by loving and sympathetic hearts, and find herself a greater favorite than she would be were she beautiful. A woman who is entirely beyond the reach of the jealousy of her own sex, is an exceedingly fortunate woman; and if personal homeliness has won for her this immunity, then homeliness has given her much to be thankful for. A homely woman who ignores her face and form, cultivates her mind and manners, good-naturedly gives up all pretension, and exhibits in all her life a true and a pure heart, will have friends enough to compensate her entirely for the loss of a husband. Friendship is unmindful of faces, in the selection of its objects, even if love be somewhat particular, and, sometimes, foolishly fastidious.

Life is altogether too precious a gift to be thrown away. A man who would permit a field to be overgrown with weeds and thorns simply because it would not naturally produce roses, would be very foolish, particularly if the ground should only need cultivation to enable it to yield abundantly of corn. Far be it from me to depreciate physical symmetry and personal comeliness. They are gifts of God, and they are very good; but there are better things in this world than a good face, and better things than the admiration which a good face wins. I am more and more convinced, as the years pass away, that the choicest thing this world has for a man is affection—not any special variety of affection, but the approval, the sympathy, and the devotion of true hearts. It is not necessary that this affection come from the great and the powerful. If it be genuine, that is all the heart asks. It does not criticize and graduate the value of the fountains from which it springs. It is at these fountains particularly that the unfortunates of the world are permitted to drink. They have only to accept cheerfully the conditions of their lot, and to give free and full play to all that is good and generous in them, to secure in an unusual degree the love of those into whose intimate society Providence has thrown them.

It is stated by Dr. Livingstone, the celebrated explorer of Africa, that the blow of a lion's paw upon his shoulder, which was so severe as to break his arm, completely annihilated fear; and he suggests that it is possible that Providence has mercifully arranged, that all those beasts that prey upon life shall have power to destroy the sting of death in the animals which are their natural victims. I do not believe that this power is mercifully assigned to beasts of prey alone, but that the misfortunes that assail our limbs and forms, in whatever shape and at whatever time they may come, bring with them something which lightens the blow, or obviates the pain, if we will accept it. There is a calm consciousness in every soul, however harshly the lion's paw may fall upon the body which it inhabits, that it is itself invulnerable—that whatever may be the condition of the body, the soul cannot be injured by physical forms or forces.

Physical calamity never comes with the power to extinguish that which is essential to the highest manhood and womanhood, and never fails to bring with it a motive for the adjustment of the soul to its conditions. The little boy whose "Hail Columbia" has been ringing in my ears all day, accepted the conditions of his life, and the sting of his calamity has departed. It is pleasant to say to him, and to all the brotherhood and sisterhood of ugliness and lameness, that there is every reason to believe that there is no such thing in heaven as a one-legged or a club-footed soul—no such thing as an ugly or a misshapen soul—no such thing as a blind or a deaf soul—no such thing as a soul with tainted blood in its veins; and that out of these imperfect bodies will spring spirits of consummate perfection and angelic beauty—a beauty chastened and enriched by the humiliations that were visited upon their earthly habitation.

LESSON III.

ANIMAL CONTENT.

"By sports like these are all their cares beguiled;
The sports of children satisfy the child."
GOLDSMITH.

"Ay, give me back the joyous hours
When I, myself, was ripening too;
When song, the fount, flung up its showers
Of beauty, ever fresh and new."
GOETHE'S FAUST.

I HAVE been watching a family of kittens, engaged in their exquisitely graceful play. Near them lay their mother, stretched at her length upon the flagging, taking her morning nap, and warming herself in the sun. She had eaten her breakfast, (provided by no care of her own, but at my expense,) had seen her little family fed, and having nothing further to attend to, had gone off into a doze. What a blessed freedom from care! Think of a family of four children, with no frocks to be made for them, no hair to brush, no shoes to provide, no socks to knit and mend, no school-books to buy, and no nurse! Think of a living being with the love of offspring in her bosom, and a multitude of marvellous instincts in her nature, yet knowing nothing of God, thinking not of the future, without a hope or an expectation, or a doubt or a fear, passing straight on to annihilation! At the threshold of this destiny the little kittens were carelessly playing; and they are doubtless still playing, while I write. They have no lessons to learn, they do not have to go to Sunday-school, they entertain no prejudices, except against dogs which occasionally dodge into the yard; and I judge, by the familiar way in which they play with their mother's ears, and pounce upon her tail, that they are not in any degree oppressed by a sense of the respect due to a parent. Cat and kittens will eat, and frolic, and sleep, through their brief life, and then they will curl up in some dark corner and die.

I remember that in one of the late Mr. Joseph C. Neal's "Charcoal Sketches," he puts into the mouth of a very sad and seedy loafer the expression of a wish that he were a pig, and a statement of the reasons for the wish. These reasons, as I recall them, related to the freedom of the pig from the peculiar trials and troubles of humanity. Pigs do not have to work for a living; they undertake no enterprizes, and of course fail in none; they eat and sleep through a period of months, and then come the knife and a grunt, and that is the last of them. Now I suppose this thought of Mr. Neal's loafer has been shared by millions of men. Not that everybody has at some time in his life wished he were a pig, but that nearly everybody who has had his share of the troubles and responsibilities of life, has looked upon simple animal carelessness and content with a certain degree of envy. It is not necessary to go among brutes for instances of this animal content. It can be found among men. Who does not know good-natured, ignorant, healthy fellows, who will work all day in the field, whistle all the way homeward, eat hugely of course food, sleep like logs, and take no more interest in the great questions which agitate the most of us, than the pigs they feed, and that, in return, feed them? Who has not sighed, as he has seen how easily the simple wants of certain simple natures are supplied? I remember an old man who quite unexpectedly was drafted into the grand jury, which sat in the county town less than ten miles distant from his home; and this was the great event of his life. He never tired of talking about it—(never tired himself, I mean,) and a stranger could not carry on a conversation with him for five minutes, without hearing of something which occurred when "I was in Blanktown, on the Grand Jury." It is doubtful whether Napoleon ever contemplated a victory with the complacent satisfaction that filled my old friend when he alluded to his connection with "the *grand* jury," and emphasized the adjective which magnified the jury and glorified him.

I confess that, when I pass through a rural town, and see the laborers among the corn, and the boys driving their cattle, and the girls busy in the dairies, and life passing away quietly, I cannot avoid a twinge of regret that it would be impossible for me to be content with the kind of life that I see around me, especially as I know that there is one kind of pleasure—negative, perhaps, rather than positive—which that kind of life enjoys, and in which I can never share. Relief from great responsibilities, and contentment with humble clothing, humble fare, humble society, humble aims and ambitions, humble means and humble labors—ah! how many weary, overloaded men—how many disappointed hearts—have sighed for such a boon, and sighed knowing they could never receive it.

It has been the habit of poets to surround simple pleasures and pursuits with the golden atmosphere of romance,—not because they would enjoy such pleasures and pursuits at all, but rather because they are forever beyond their possession. A poet is always reaching toward the unattainable, and he may reach forward to the perfections of a life of which the best that he sees around him is an intimation, or backward to the animal content of a life as yet undisturbed by the intimation of something better. Bucolics are very sweet, but their writers do not believe in them. "A nut-brown maid," with bare, unconscious feet and ancles, is very pretty in a picture, but the man who painted her ascertained that she was green, and not the most entertaining of companions. The truth is, that when we have got along so far that we can perceive that which is poetical and picturesque in the simplest form of rustic life, we have got too far along to enjoy it.

I suppose that much of the charm which simple animal content has for us, is connected with the memories of childhood. We can all recall a period of our lives when there was joy in the consciousness of living—when animal life, in its spontaneous overflow, flooded all our careless hours with its own peculiar pleasure. The light was pleasant to our eyes, vigorous appetite and digestion made ambrosia of the homeliest fare, the simplest play brought delight, and life—all untried—lay spread out before us in one long, golden dream. We now watch our children at their sports, and see but little difference between their sources of happiness and those which supply the kittens in their play. "Pleased with a rattle, tickled with a straw," they skip from pleasure to pleasure, and find delight in the impulsive exercise of their little powers. We were once like them. Life was once as fresh, and flowing, and impulsive, and objectless, as it is with them; and when we are weary and oppressed with labor, and loaded down with responsibility, and filled with thoughts of the great destiny before us, we turn our eyes backward with a sigh for days once ours, but lost forever. Lost forever! This is the romantic pain that fills us in all our contemplations of simple animal content. It is lost to us, because we are lost to it. Like a passenger far out upon the sea, adventuring upon a long voyage, we look back upon the fading hills of our native land, and sigh to think that the breeze which bears us away can never bring us back.

The question comes to us: "What is there in our present life to repay us for this loss?" There are multitudes who can ask this question, and answer honestly, "Nothing." It is sad, but true, that countless men and women have never found any thing in life which compensates them for the loss of the simple animal enjoyment and content of childhood. Sickness, perhaps, has imposed upon them years of pain. Poverty has condemned them to labor through every waking hour to win sustenance for themselves and their dependents. The heart has been cheated of its idol. Friends have proved false, and fortune fickle. Life has gone wrong through all the avenues of their being. Yet there are others who, while looking with pleasure upon the innocent sports of animal life, and recalling the simple joys of childhood with delight, are content with the lot of manhood and womanhood, and would look upon a return to their simpler age as the greatest calamity that could be inflicted upon them. With brows wrinkled by care and toil, and heads silvered by premature age, and great burdens upon heart and brain, they glory in a life within and before them, by the side of which the life of childhood is as flavorless and frivolous as that of a fly.

I have been much impressed by a passage in the "Recreations of a Country Parson,"—which, by the way, is one of the best and cleverest books of its kind in the English language—in which this question is incidentally touched upon, and so happily touched upon, that I cannot refrain from transcribing the whole passage. The writer represents himself to be seated upon a manger, writing upon the flat place between his horse's eyes, while the docile animal's nose is between his knees; and it is the horse that he addresses:—

"For you, my poor fellow-creature, I think with sorrow as I write here upon your head, there remains no such immortality as remains for me. What a difference between us! You to your sixteen or eighteen years here, and then oblivion!—I to my threescore and ten, and then eternity! Yes, the difference is immense; and it touches me to think of your life and mine, of your doom and mine. I know a house where at morning and evening prayer, when the household assembles, among the servants there always walks in a shaggy little dog, who listens with the deepest attention and the most solemn gravity to all that is said, and then, when prayers are over, goes out again with his friends. I cannot witness that silent procedure without being much moved by the sight. Ah! my fellow-creature, this is something in which you have no part! Made by the same hand, breathing the same air, sustained like us by food and drink, you are witnessing an act of ours which relates to interests that do not concern you, and of which you have no idea. And so here we are, you standing at the manger, old boy, and I sitting upon it; the mortal and the immortal, close together; your nose on my knee, my paper on your head; yet with something between us broader than the broad Atlantic."

Here we find one man pitying his poor, dumb, unconscious companion, and the little dog that trots in to attend the morning prayers, because their life is so brief, and, more particularly, because it is so insignificant. He recognizes the feeble likeness between himself and them, and appreciates also the tremendous difference. He does not think that he would be glad to exchange his lot of labor and care for their carelessness and content, but, reaching forward to grasp the hand of an immortal destiny, he sorrows that he must leave his dumb servants and companions behind him.

And this is the normal view of the question. We rise out of semi-conscious infancy into a life of the senses, which goes on to perfection in our childhood. We come into a state in which the mechanism of the body enjoys its freest play, in which the senses imbibe their sweetest satisfactions, and in which life either swells into irrepressible overflowings, or subsides into careless content. Looking at her children at this period of their life, many a mother has said, "Let them play while they can; let them be merry while they may; for they are seeing their happiest days." But this animal life is not all. In its perfection it is very beautiful, and it is good because God made it; but it is only the coarse basis upon which rises a shaft, whiter than marble—wrought with divine devices—crowned by the light of Heaven. It is only those who have failed to secure a distinct perception of the highest aspect of human life, and of that which makes it characteristically human life, who can say to a child that he is seeing his happiest days.

I remember with entire distinctness the moment when the consciousness possessed me that my childhood was transcended by initial manhood, and I can never forget the pang that moment brought me. It was on a bright, moonlight night, in midwinter, when my mates, boisterous with life, were engaged in their usual games in the snow, and I had gone out expecting to share in their enjoyment. I had not played, or rather tried to play, five minutes, before I found that there was nothing in the play for me—that I had absolutely exhausted play as the grand pursuit of my life. Never since has the wild laugh of boyhood sounded so vacant and hollow, as it did to me that night. In an instant, the invisible line was crossed which separated a life of purely animal enjoyment from a life of moral motive and responsibility, and intellectual action and enterprise. The old had passed away, and I had entered that which was new; and I turned my steps homeward, leaving behind me all my companions, to spend a quiet evening in the chimney-corner, and dream of the realm that was opening before me. Such a moment as this comes really, though not always consciously, to every man and woman. To-day we are children; to-morrow we are not. To-day we stand in life's vestibule; to-morrow we are in the temple, awed by the sweep of the arches over us, humbled by the cross that fronts us, and smitten with mysteries that breathe upon us from the choir, or gaze at us from the flaming windows.

Manhood and womanhood have their infancy entirely distinct from the infancy of childhood. The child is born into the world a simple, animal life—less helpful than a lamb, or a calf, or a kitten. There is no power in it, and but little of instinct. There is no form of life, bursting caul or shell, that awakes in vital air to such stupid, vacant helplessness, as a baby. It is out of this lump of clay, with its bones only half hardened, and its muscles little more than pulp, and its brain no more intelligent than an uncooked dumpling, that childhood is to be made. And this childhood consists of little more than a well-developed animal organism. Nature keeps the child playing—makes it play in the open air—impels it to bring into free and joyous use all the powers of its little frame—and when that is done, and the procreative faculty has crowned all, the child is born again, and comes into a new infancy—the infancy of manhood and womanhood. Here a new life opens. That which gave satisfaction before, gives satisfaction no longer. Love takes new and deeper channels. Ambition fixes its eye upon other and higher objects. Fresh motives address the soul, and urge it into new enterprises. Great cares and responsibilities settle slowly down upon its shoulders, and it braces itself up to endure them. It apprehends God and its relations to Him, and to its fellows; it confronts destiny; it arms itself for the conflicts of life; it prepares for the struggle which it knows will issue in a grateful success or a sad disappointment; in short, it grows from man's infancy into man's full estate.

Now the reason why a mother looks with a sigh upon her children, and says that they are seeing the happiest days of their life, is that she has never become a true woman. She has never grown out of the infancy of her womanhood. She has never comprehended what a glorious thing it is to be a woman—she has not comprehended what it is to be a woman at all. What can be that woman's ideas of life, who thinks and declares that the happiest moments of her experience were those which were filled with the frolic of animal life? If I felt like this, I should wish that my children had been born rabbits, or squirrels, or lambs, or kittens, because they, having enjoyed the pleasures of the animal, will never awake to the woes of another type of life. The real reason why any man sings from the heart,

"O, would I were a boy again,"

is, that he is "stuck"—to use a homely but expressive word—between boyhood and manhood, and, not feeling up to his position, has a very strong disposition to back out of it. The man who really wishes he were a boy, is either painfully conscious of the loss of the purity of his boyhood, or he has the cowardly disposition to shirk the responsibilities of his life. The romantic regard which we all entertain for the simple animal content and joy of childhood, is a very different thing to this. It was Mr. Neal's loafer that really wished he were a pig; and it is a loafer always who would retire from man's duties and estate, into the content either of childhood or kittenhood.

It is very natural that a man should be blinded and pained by passing from a shaded room into dazzling sunlight. It is a serious thing to leap from a luxurious, enervating warm bath into cold water. All sudden transitions are shocking; and God has contrived the transitions of our lives so that they shall be mainly gradual. It is not to be wondered at that many men and women, by having the responsibilities of men and women thrust upon them too early, are shocked, and look back upon the shady places they have left, and long to rest their eyes there. It is not strange that men recoil from a plunge into the world's cold waters, and long to creep back into the bath from which they have suddenly risen. But that man or woman, having fully passed into the estate of man and woman, should desire to become children again, is impossible. It is only the half-developed, the badly-developed, the imperfectly nurtured, the mean-spirited, and the demoralized, who look back to the innocence, the helplessness, and the simple animal joy and content of childhood with genuine regret for their loss. I want no better evidence that a person's life is regarded by himself as a failure, than that furnished by his honest willingness to be restored to his childhood. When a man is ready to relinquish the power of his mature reason, his strength and skill for self-support, the independence of his will and life, his bosom companion and children, his interest in the stirring affairs of his time, his part in deciding the great questions which agitate his age and nation, his intelligent apprehension of the relations which exist between himself and his Maker, and his rational hope of immortality—if he have one—for the negative animal content, and frivolous enjoyments of a child, he does not deserve the name of a man;—he is a weak, unhealthy, broken-down creature, or a base poltroon.

Yet I know there are those who will read this sentence with tears, and with complaint. I know there are those whose existence has been a long struggle with sickness and trial—whose lives have been crowded with great griefs and disappointments—who sit in darkness and impotency while the world rolls by them. They have seen no joy and felt no content since childhood, and many of them look with genuine pity upon children, because the careless creatures do not know into what a heritage of sin and sorrow they are entering. I have only to say to them, that the noblest exhibitions of manhood and womanhood I have ever seen, or the world has ever seen, have been among their number. A woman with the hope of heaven in her eyes, incorruptible virtue in her heart, and honesty in every endeavor, has smiled serenely, a million times in this world, while her life and all its earthly expectations were in ruins. Patient sufferers upon beds of pain have forgotten childhood years ago, and, feeding their souls on prayer, have looked forward with unutterable joy to the transition from womanhood to angelhood. Men, utterly forsaken by friends—contemned, derided, proscribed, persecuted—have stood by their convictions with joyful heroism and calm content. Nay, great multitudes have marched with songs upon their tongues to the rack and the stake. The noblest spectacle the world affords is that of a man or woman, rising superior to sorrow and suffering—transforming sorrow and suffering into nutriment—accepting those conditions of their life which Providence prescribes, and building themselves up into an estate from whose summit the step is short to a glorified humanity.

Before me hangs the portrait of an old man—the only man I ever loved with a devotion that has never faded, though long years have passed away since he died. His calm blue eyes look down upon me, and I look into them, and through them I look into a golden memory—into a life of self-denial—into a meek, toiling, honest, heroic Christian manhood—into an uncomplaining spirit—into a grateful heart—into a soul that never sighed over a lost joy, though all his earthly enterprises miscarried. The tracery of care and of sickness is upon his haggard features, but I see in them, and in the soul which they represent to me, the majesty of manliness. While I look, the kittens still play at the door, and the noise of shouting children is in the street; but ah! how shallow is the life they represent, compared with that of which this dumb canvas tells me! It is better to be a man or a woman, than to be a child. It is better to be an angel than to be either. Let us look forward—never backward.

LESSON IV.

REPRODUCTION IN KIND.

"Whatsoever a man soweth, that shall he also reap."
St. Paul to the Galatians.

"Ye shall know them by their fruits: Do men gather grapes of thorns, or figs of thistles?"—St. Matthew's Gospel.

IT was fitting that one of the most characteristic and beautiful laws of life should be announced in the opening chapter of the Holy Bible. It was clothed in the form of an ordinance, as became it: "Let the earth bring forth the living creature after his kind, and every thing that creepeth upon the earth, after his kind." From that day to this, every living thing—beast, bird and insect, tree, shrub and plant—has produced after its kind. It is a law that runs through all animal and vegetable life. Each family in the great world of living forms was created for a special purpose, and was intended to remain pure and distinctive until the termination of its mission. Whenever the family boundaries are overstepped, the curse of nature is breathed upon the generative functions, and the illegitimate product dies out, or subsides into hopeless degeneration. The mule is a monster, and has no progeny.

A plant, or a tree, never forgets itself. Cheat it of its root, and the stem remains faithful. The minutest twig, put out to nurse upon the arm of a foreign mother, feels the thrill of the great primal law in its filmiest fibre, and breathes in every expression of its life its fidelity. If you will walk with me into the garden, I will show you a mountain-ash in full bloom; but on the top of it you will see a strange little cluster of pear-blossoms. A twig from a Seckel pear-tree was, two or three years since, engrafted there. It had a hard time in uniting its being to that of the alien ash, but it loved life, and so, at length, it consented to join itself to the transplanted forest tree. It was weak and alone, but it kept its law. Spring bathed the ash with its own peculiar bloom, and autumn hung it with its clusters of scarlet berries, and it was hidden from sight by the redundant foliage, but it kept its law. The roots of the mountain-ash, blindly reaching in the ground and imbibing its juices, knew nothing of the little orphaned twig above, that waited for its food; but they could not cheat it of its law. Up to a certain point of a certain bough the rising fluids came under the law of the mountain-ash, and there they found a gateway, guarded by an angel that gave them a new commandment. "Thus far—mountain-ash: beyond—Seckel pear;" and if, in October, you will walk in the garden again with me, I will show you among the scarlet berries, bending heavily toward you, the clustered succulence of the Seckel.

A seedsman may cheat you, but a seed never does. If you plant corn, it never comes up potatoes. If you sow wheat, it never comes up rye. Wrapped up in every capsule, bound up in every kernel, packed into every minutest germ, is this law, written by God at the beginning, "Produce thou after thy kind." So the whole living world goes on producing after its kind. Year after year we visit the seedsman, and read the labels on his drawers and packages, and bear home and plant in our gardens the little homely germs that keep God's law so well; and summer rewards our trust in them with beautiful flowers, and autumn with bountiful fruition. Robins sang the same song to the Pilgrim Fathers that they sing to us. The may-flower breathes the same fragrance now that it breathed in the fingers of Rose Standish; and man and woman, producing after their kind, are the same to-day that they were three thousand years ago.

Now there is a significance in all the laws of material life, above and beyond their special office. They do the work they were set to do; they rule the life they were appointed to rule; but the laws, themselves, belong to a family whose branches run through all intellectual, moral, and spiritual life. Laws live in groups no less uniformly than the existences which they inform and govern. It is a law, both of animal and vegetable structures, that they shall grow by what they feed on; but this law passes the bounds of matter, and finds its widest meaning and its most extended application beyond. The mind grows by what it feeds on; the heart grows by what it feeds on; love, hate, jealousy, revenge, fortitude, courage, grow by what they feed on; spirituality grows by what spirituality feeds on. Wherever growth goes, through all the realm of God, this law goes; and the law that every thing that produces shall produce after its kind, is just as universal as this. It begins in material life, and runs up through all life. Rather, perhaps, I should say, that it begins in spiritual life, and seeks embodiment in material life, so that we may apprehend it. The clouds were in heaven before there was any rain, and the rain comes down from heaven to tell us what the clouds are made of. I might go further, and say that every form of matter is but the embodiment of a divine thought, and that, with that thought, there passes into matter the laws that reside in divine things of corresponding nature and office.

But I am becoming abstruse—quite too much so, considering the simple, practical truths to which I am seeking to introduce my reader. I have been thinking how, in accordance with this law of which we are talking, our moods, our passions, our sympathies, our moral frames and conditions, reproduce themselves, after their kind, in the minds and lives around us. I call my child to my knee in anger; I strike him a hasty blow that carries with it the peculiar sting of anger; I speak a loud reproof that bears with it the spirit of anger; and I look in vain for any relenting in his flashing eyes, flushed face, and compressed lips. I have made my child angry, and my uncontrolled passion has produced after its kind. I have sown anger, and I have reaped anger instantaneously. Perhaps I become still more angry, in consequence of the passion manifested by my child, and I speak and strike again. He is weak and I am strong; but, though he bow his head, crushed into silence, I may be sure that there is a sullen heart in the little bosom, and anger the more bitter because it is impotent. I put the child away from me, and think of what I have done. I am full of relentings. I long to ask his pardon, for I know that I have offended and deeply injured one of Christ's little ones. I call him to me again, press his head to my breast, kiss him, and weep. No word is spoken, but the little bosom heaves, the little heart softens, the little eyes grow tenderly penitent, the little hands come up and clasp my neck, and my relentings and my sorrow have produced after their kind. The child is conquered, and so am I.

If I utter fretful words, they come back to me like echoes. If I bristle all over with irritability, the quills will begin to rise all about me. One thoroughly irritable person in a breakfast-room spoils coffee and toast, sours milk, and destroys appetite for a whole family. He produces after his kind.

Generally, a man has around him those who are like him. If he be a man of strong nature and positive qualities, he will plant his moods and grow them in the natures next to him. Of course there must be exceptions to this rule, because the will is free and man is reasonable, and the motive and power to pluck up unwelcome seed, and unpleasant growths, inheres in all men. I have known a good-natured man to live with a pettish, ill-natured, jealous, fault-finding wife through all the years of my acquaintance with him, he meantime growing no worse, and she growing no better. They had voluntarily and effectually shut themselves each from the influence of the other. He had closed his spirit against that which was bad in her, and she had closed her spirit against that which was good in him; so she went on fretting through life, and he very good-naturedly laughing at her. We see this thing through all society. We see innocent girls grow up into virtue, though surrounded on every side by vicious example. We see natures and characters everywhere which refuse to receive the seed that falls upon them from the natures and characters of others; but this makes nothing against the universality of the law we are considering. Generally, I repeat, a man has around him those who are like him. The soil of a social circle is usually open, and whatever falls into it produces after its kind, whether it be good nature or ill nature, purity or impurity, faith or skepticism, love or hate.

It would appear, therefore, that there is no way by which we can surround ourselves by good society so readily as by being good ourselves. If we plant good seed, we may calculate with a great degree of certainty upon securing good fruit. If I plant frankness and open-heartedness, I expect to reap them; and I have no right to expect to reap them unless I plant them. If I go to a man with my heart in my hand, I have good reason for expecting to meet a man with his heart in his hand. Frankness begets frankness, just as naturally and just as certainly, under the proper conditions, as like produces like in the animal and vegetable kingdoms. There are men who do every thing by indirection; who meet one as warily as if words were traps; and pitfalls who manage a friendly interview as a general would manage a campaign; and if they make their demonstration first, we are placed upon our guard.

We unconsciously become wary and distrustful. They plant distrust and secretiveness, and they produce in us after their kind. No man can be treated frankly in this world unless he himself be frank. If we would win confidence to ourselves, we must put confidence in others. The soul is like a mirror, reflecting that which stands before it.

The young naturally take on the moods and accept and reflect the influences around them more readily than the old, just as a new piece of land will produce a better crop than one which is worn or pre-occupied. A virgin mind is like a virgin soil. It contains all the elements of fertility, and is adapted to the production of any crop. It has been exhausted in no department of its constitution. It is not occupied by roots, and shaded by foliage. It is not turf-bound and dry; but it is soft and open, and clean and moist, and ready for the reception of any seed that may fall upon it. Until age brings individuality, the mind seems to have little choice as to what it will receive. Then, indeed, it does reject much seed that falls upon it, and much fails to take root because of the pre-occupation of the surface. A sensual seed is planted in the soul of a young man, and it springs up readily, and produces after its kind; but the same seed tossed upon an older soil fails to sink and germinate, because the surface is pre-occupied, or, more frequently, because that peculiar element on which the germ must rely for quickening and sustentation has been exhausted. Some manly or Christian grace falls upon a young mind, and quickly strikes root and rises into flower and fruit, while the same grace thrown upon an adult mind would fail to reach the soil, through the vices that cumber and choke it. It is thus that home and the school-room are literally seminaries —places where seed is sown—and it is in these that we expect and intend that every seed shall produce after its kind. Let us talk about this a little.

I once heard a person say that one of his acquaintances, whom he named, had no moral right to have a child. Why was this harsh judgment uttered? Because he was hereditarily scrofulous, and would necessarily entail upon his offspring the family taint. If there were even a show of justice in this, what must be said of a parent who does not possess a single moral quality, that even he, in the selfishness of his parental love, would desire to see implanted in his child? How many homes are scattered over Christendom in which no good seed is sown! How many selfish, niggardly, vicious parents are there, who, producing after their kind, by generation and by influence, are filling the world with selfish, niggardly, and vicious children! How many homes are there in which the gentle words of love are never heard; in which the tender graces of a Christian heart are never unfolded; in which a prayer is never uttered! How many fathers are there whose lips are black with profanity and foul with obscenity, and whose lives are mean and unwholesome! How many mothers are there whose tongues are nimble with scandal and bitter with scolding, and whose brains are busy with vanities and jealousies! Ah! if there be any man or woman in this world who has no moral right to have a child, it is one who has not a single trait of character desirable to be reproduced in a child. Scrofula may be bad, but sin is worse. Bodily taint may be terrible, but spiritual taint is horrible.

It is a general truth, under the law that every thing produces after its kind, that children become what their parents are. A simple people, virtuous and healthy, will produce virtuous, healthy, and true-hearted children. A luxurious people—lazy, sensual, wasteful—will produce children like themselves. If we go through the vicious quarters of a great city, where licentiousness and drunkenness and beastly vices prevail, we shall find that though all die before old age, the communities are abundantly recruited by the children which they produce. Men, principles, habits, ideas, vices, all have children, whose features betray their parentage; so that no parent has a right to expect a child to be better than its father and mother. On the contrary, he has every reason to believe that every thing that a child sees wrong in the parents, will be imitated. There is no way by which bad parents can bring up a family well. There must be in the parental life good principles, a sweet and equable temper, a tender and loving disposition, a firm self-control, a pleasant deportment, and a conscientious devotion to duty, or these will not be found in the life of the children. Bad seed, sown in the quick soil of a child's mind, is sure to spring up, and to bear fruit after its kind. No sensible man ever dreams of gathering figs from thistles, or grapes from bramble-bushes, and no man has the slightest right to suppose that he can bring up a family to be better than he is. The plant will be true to the seed.

We are in the habit of hearing that the children of a certain neighborhood, or school, or town, are extraordinarily bad children. Great wonder is sometimes expressed in regard to such instances, when, really, they are not wonderful at all. When children are unusually bad, parents are unusually bad, or, if they are not bad-hearted, they are wrong-headed. I ought, perhaps, to say here that I have known an irascible, tyrannical, unjust and cruel school-teacher to spoil a neighborhood of children, when the parents were without any special fault, save that of failing to thrust him out of the charge which he had abused. But usually the fault is at home. If the seed planted there be good, it will produce good fruit. Yet my reader will say that the best man he ever knew, had the worst children he ever saw. The truth of the statement is admitted, but what do you know of the home life of that family? How much unreasonable restraint has been exercised upon those children? From how many exhibitions of stern and unrelenting injustice have these children suffered? What laxity of discipline and carelessness of culture have reigned in that family? I know many who seem to be excellent men in society, but who are any thing but amiable men at home. In one they are pleasant, affable, kind, and charitable; in the other, cross-grained, hard, unkind, and unjust. I declare with all positiveness, that when a family or a neighborhood of children is bad, there is a reason for it outside of the children. There are bad influences which descend upon them, and work out their natural results in them.

It is astonishing to see how long a seed will lie in the ground without germinating, and how true it will remain to its kind through untold years. Cut down a pine forest, where an oak has not been seen for a century, and oak shrubbery will spring up. Heave out upon the surface a pile of earth that has lain hidden from the eyes of a dozen generations, and forthwith it will grow green with weeds. Plough up the prairie, and turn under the grass and flowers that have grown there since the white settler can remember, and there will spring from the inverted sod a strange growth that has had no representative in the sunlight for long ages. Soul and soil are alike in this. I once heard a man say of his father, who had been dead many years —"I hate him: I hate his memory." The words were spoken bitterly, with a flushed face and angry eyes, yet he who spoke them was one of the kindest and most placable of men. Deep down in his heart, under love for his mother which was almost worship, and under affection for wife, children, and sisters which was as deep as his nature, and under multiplied friendships, there had been planted this seed. The father had treated the boy harshly and unjustly; and the young soul was stung as the tender fruit is stung by an insect. Where anger and resentment were sown, anger and resentment were ready to spring up the moment the seed was uncovered. I have known men to carry through life a revenge planted in their hearts by some unjust and cruel schoolmaster. How many men are there are in the world who have sworn to revenge themselves upon one who had stung them with anger or injustice when in childhood!

So we come to the grand lesson, that if we would have good children, we must ourselves be exactly what we would have them become; if we would govern our families, we must first govern ourselves; if we would have only pleasant words greet our ears in the home circle, we must speak only pleasant words. We should see to it that we plant nothing, the legitimate fruits of which we shall not be willing and glad to see borne in the lives of our children. If our children are bad, the fault is, ninety-nine cases in a hundred, our own, in some way. If we would reform society, or make it better in any respect, our quickest way to do it is to reform and make ourselves better. If I would reap courtesy and hospitality and kindness and love, I must plant them; and it is the sum of all arrogance to assume that I have a right to reap them without planting them. A man who receives courtesy without exercising it, reaps that which he has not sown. He is a thief, and ought in justice to be kicked out of society. Blessings on the man who sows the seeds of a happy nature and a noble character broadcast wherever his feet wander,—who has a smile alike for joy and sorrow, a tender word always for a child, a compassionate utterance for suffering, courtesy for friends and for strangers, encouragement for the despairing, an open heart for all—love for all—good words for all! Such seed produces after its kind in all soils, when it finds lodgment; and that which the sower fails to reap, passes into hands that are grateful for the largess.

LESSON V.

TRUTH AND TRUTHFULNESS.

For truth is as impossible to be soiled by any outward touch as a sunbeam."
MILTON.

"Odds life! must one swear to the truth of a song?"—MATTHEW PRIOR.

"Get but the truth once uttered, and 'tis like
A star new-born that drops into its place,
And which, once circling in its placid round,
Not all the tumult of the earth can shake."—LOWELL.

ONE of the rarest powers possessed by man is the power to state a fact. It seems a very simple thing to tell the truth, but, beyond all question, there is nothing half so easy as lying. To comprehend a fact in its exact length, breadth, relations, and significance, and to state it in language that shall represent it with exact fidelity, are the work of a mind singularly gifted, finely balanced, and thoroughly practiced in that special department of effort. The greatness of Daniel Webster was more apparent in his power to state a fact, or to present a truth, than in any other characteristic of his gigantic nature. It was the power of truth that won for him his forensic victories. Whenever he was truest to truth, then was truth truest to him. He was a man who implicitly believed in the power of truth to take care of itself when it had been fairly presented; and the failures of his life always grew out of his attempts to make falsehood look like truth—a field of effort in which the most gifted of his cotemporaries won the most brilliant of his triumphs.

The men are comparatively few who are in the habit of telling the truth. We all lie, every day of our lives—almost in every sentence we utter—not consciously and criminally, perhaps, but really, in that our language fails to represent truth, and state facts correctly. Our truths are half-truths, or distorted truths, or exaggerated truths, or sophisticated truths. Much of this is owing to carelessness, much to habit, and, more than has generally been supposed, to mental incapacity. I have known eminent men who had not the power to state a fact, in its whole volume and outline, because, first, they could not comprehend it perfectly, and, second, because their power of expression was limited. The lenses by which they apprehended their facts were not adjusted properly, so they saw every thing with a blur. Definite outlines, cleanly cut edges, exact apprehension of volume and weight, nice measurement of relations, were matters outside of their observation and experience. They had broad minds, but bungling; and their language was no better than their apprehensions—usually it was worse, because language is rarely as definite as apprehension. Men rarely do their work to suit them, because their tools are imperfect.

There are men in all communities who are believed to be honest, yet whose word is never taken as authority upon any subject. There is a flaw or a warp somewhere in their perceptions, which prevents them from receiving truthful impressions. Every thing comes to them distorted, as natural objects are distorted by reaching the eye through wrinkled window-glass. Some are able to apprehend a fact and state it correctly, if it have no direct relation to themselves; but the moment their personality, or their personal interest, is involved, the fact assumes false proportions and false colors. I know a physician whose patients are always alarmingly sick when he is first called to them. As they usually get well, I am bound to believe that he is a good physician; but I am not bound to believe that they are all as sick at beginning as he supposes them to be. The first violent symptoms operate upon his imagination and excite his fears, and his opinion as to the degree of danger attaching to the diseases of his patients is not worth half so much as that of any sensible old nurse. In fact, nobody thinks of taking it all; and those who know him, and who hear his sad representations of the condition of his patients, show equal distrust of his word and faith in his skill, by taking it for granted that they are in a fair way to get well.

It is impossible for bigots, for men of one idea, for fanatics, for those who set boundaries to themselves in religious, social, and political creeds, for men who think more of their own selfish interests than they do of truth, and for vicious men, to speak the truth. We are all, I suppose, bigots to a greater or less extent. We all have a creed written in our minds, or printed in our books; and to this we are more or less blindly attached. We set down an article of faith, or adopt an opinion, and nothing is allowed to interfere with it. If a sturdy fact comes along, and asks admission, we turn to our creed to see if we can safely entertain it. If the creed says "No," we say "No," and the fact is turned out of doors, and misrepresented after it is gone. Our creeds are our dwellings. They come next to us, and nothing can come to us, or go out from us, without going through our creeds. The simple fact of the death of Jesus Christ upon the cross, reaching the mind through various creeds, and passing out again, goes through as many phases as there are creeds, ranging through a scale which at one extreme presents a God dying to redeem the lost millions of a world, and, at the other, a benevolent, sweet-tempered man, yielding his life in testimony of the honesty of his teachings.

No new truth presents itself, which does not have to run the gauntlet of our creeds. If it get through alive, and seem disposed to be peaceable, and to remain subordinate to them, then we let it live, and receive it into respectable society;—otherwise, we entreat it shamefully. Sometimes the truth is too much for us, and asserts its power to stand without our help, and then we compromise with it. The world will turn on its axis, and wheel around its orbit, though we stop the mouth of the profane wretch who declares it; so, after a while, we get tired of fighting the fact, and shape our creeds accordingly. We fight the sturdy truths of geology, because they interfere with our creeds, but after awhile the sturdy truths of geology become too sturdy for us, and then we begin to patronize them, and to confer upon them the honor of harmonizing with our creeds. A man who has adopted the creed of a materialist, is entirely incompetent to receive, entertain, and represent a spiritual fact. My creed is the window at which I sit, and look at all the world of truth outside of me. All truth is tinted by the medium through which it passes to reach my mind; and such is my imperfection and my weakness, that I could not raise my window immediately, and place my soul in direct, vital contact with the great atmosphere of truth, if I would.

But if bigotry be such a bar to the correct perception of truth, what shall be said of self-interest and personal vices of appetite and passion? It is possible for no man who owns a slave and finds profit in such ownership, to receive the truth touching the right of man to himself, and the moral wrong of slavery. We have too much evidence that even creeds must bend to self-interest, and that any traffic will be regarded as morally right which is pecuniarily profitable. Once, in the creed of the slaveholders, slavery was admitted to be wrong, but that was when it was looked upon as temporary in its character, and, on the whole, evil in its results to all concerned. Now, when it is sought to be made a permanent institution, because it seems to be the only source of the wealth of a section, it has become right; and even the slave-trade logically falls into the category of laudable and legitimate commerce. It is impossible for a people who have allowed pecuniary interest to deprave their moral sense to this extent, to perceive and receive any sound political truth, or to apprehend the spirit and temper of those who are opposed to them. The same may be said of the liquor traffic. The act of selling liquor is looked upon with horror by those who stand outside, and who have an eye upon its consequences; but the seller deems it legitimate, and looks upon any interference with his sales as an infringement of his rights. Our selfish interest in any business, or in any scheme of profit, distorts all truth either directly or indirectly related to such business or scheme, or living in its region and atmosphere. The President of the United States, or the governor of the commonwealth, may be an excellent man; but if I want an office, and he fails to appoint me to it, why I don't exactly regard him as such. He becomes to me a very ordinary and vulgar sort of man indeed; but if he give me my office, then, though he may be all that his enemies think him, he seems to me to be invested with a singular nobility of character that other people do not apprehend at all.

The vices of humanity are sad media through which to receive truth—often so opaque that no truth can reach the mind at all. It is impossible for a man whose affections are bestialized, whose practices are libertine, and whose imaginations are all impure, to receive the truth that there are such things as purity and virtue, and that there are men and women around him who are virtuous and pure. There is no truth which personal vice will not distort. The approaches to a sensual mind are through the senses, and the same may be said of all minds in a general way; but the approaches to a sensual mind are only through the senses, and they, being perverted, abused, exhausted, or unduly excited, furnish the utterly unreliable avenues by which truth reaches the soul. The grand reason why truth, published from the pulpit and the platform, revealed in periodicals and books, and embodied in pictures and statues, works no greater changes upon the minds and morals of men, is, that it never gets inside of men in the shape in which it is uttered. It passes through such media of bigotry, or self-interest, or vice, that its identity and power are lost.

It is not, therefore, remarkable that so little truth is told when so little is received—that so little is expressed when so little is apprehended. The largest field will not produce an oat-straw that will stand alone, if there be no silica in the soil, and the largest mind cannot express a pure truth if it has lived always so encased that pure truth could not find its way into it. All truth reaches our minds through various media, by which it is more or less colored and refracted; and it is very rare that a man has the power to embody in language and utter a truth in the degree of perfection in which he received it. As I said at beginning, the power to state a fact correctly, or to express a pure truth, is among the rarest gifts of man. It never struck me that David was remarkably hasty, when he said that all men were liars. All men are liars, in one respect or another. They are divisible into various classes, which may legitimately be mentioned under two heads, viz., unconscious liars and conscious liars.

Of those who lie, and suppose they are telling the truth, I have already spoken. They are a large and most respectable class of people, and their apology must be found in the theory I have advanced; yet among these may be found men and women who will require all the amplitude of our mantles of charity to cover them. I have been much impressed with a passage in Dr. Bushnell's recent volume, entitled "Christian Nurture," which incidentally touches upon this subject, in the writer's characteristically powerful way; and as I cannot condense it, I will copy it:

"There is, in some persons who appear in all other respects to be Christian, a strange defect of truth, or truthfulness. They are not conscious of it. They would take it as a cruel injustice were they only to suspect their acquaintances of holding such an estimate of them. And yet, there is a want of truth in every sort of demonstration they make. It is not their words only that lie, but their voice, air, action; their every putting forth has a lying character. The atmosphere they live in is an atmosphere of pretence. Their virtues are affectations. Their compassions and sympathies are the airs they put on. Their friendship is their mood, and nothing more; and yet they do not know it. They mean, it may be, no fraud. They only cheat themselves so effectually as to believe that what they are only acting is their truth. And, what is difficult to reconcile, they have a great many Christian sentiments; they maintain prayer as a habit, and will sometimes speak intelligently of matters of Christian experience."

It was the oracular sage, Deacon Bedott, who, in view of the imperfections of his kind, remarked several times in his life: "we are all poor creeturs"—a remark that comes as near to being pure truth as any we meet with outside of the Bible and the standard treatises on mathematics. We are, indeed, poor creatures. Our highest conceptions of truth are contemptible, our best utterances fall short of our conceptions, and our lives are poorer than our language.

Of all conscious and criminal lying, I know of none that exceeds in malignity and magnitude that of a political campaign. In such a struggle, men get in love with lies. They seek apologies for the circulation of lies. They hug lies to their hearts in preference to truth. It is the habit of hopeful philosophers to enlarge upon the benefit to our people of the annual and quadrennial contests for place, which occur in our country, as if principles were the things really at stake, and personalities were out of the question, as the lying politicians would have us believe. What, in honesty, can be said of the leading speakers and the leading presses which sustain a party in a contest for power, but that they studiously misrepresent their opponents, misstate their own motives, give currency to false accusations, suppress truth that tells against them, exaggerate the importance of that which favors them, seize upon all plausible pretexts for fraud, skulk behind subterfuges, and lie outright when it is deemed necessary. And what can be expected more and better than this, when the leaders are office-seekers, who live and thrive on the grand basilar lie that the motive which inspires all their action is a regard for the popular good? Of course I speak generally. There are politicians and presses that are above personal considerations; but even these become infected with the prevalent poison of falsehood that is everywhere associated with their efforts.

The social lying of the world has found multitudinous satirists, and furnished the staple of a whole school of writers. We touch our hats in token of respect to men whom in our hearts we despise. We inquire tenderly for the health of persons for whom we do not care a straw. We who cannot afford it wear expensive clothing, and display grand equipage, and give costly entertainments, not because we enjoy it, but because we wish to impress upon the world the belief that we can afford it. It is our way of expressing a lie which seems to us important to the maintenance of our social standing. We receive with a kiss a visitor whom we wish were in Greenland, and betray her to the next who comes in. We pretend to ourselves and our neighbors that there is nothing which we so much esteem as the simple friendships of life, and the straight-forward love and hearty good will of the honest hearts around us, yet when the rich and the titled are near, we are gladdened and flattered, and look with supercilious contempt upon the humble friendships which we affected to cherish supremely. In our conscience and judgment, we appreciate the genuine values of social life, and we profess in our language to hold them in just estimation, but in our life and practice we honor that which is fictitious and conventional, apprehending in our conscience and judgment that we are acting a lie. Socially I cannot but believe that there is far more of truthfulness in humble than in high life. The more nearly we come down to hearty nature, and the further we go from the artificial and conventional, the nearer do we come to truth. Truth is indeed at the bottom of this well, and not in the artificial wall that rises above it, nor the buckets that go up and down as caprice or selfishness turns the windlass.

Business lying is, after all, the most universal of any. It is confined to no age and no nation. Solomon understood the world's great game when he wrote: "It is naught, it is naught, saith the buyer: but when he is gone his way, then he boasteth;" and from Solomon's day down to ours, buyers have depreciated that which they would purchase, and then boasted of their bargains. When two selfish persons meet on opposite sides of a counter, there rises between them a sort of antagonism. One is interested in selling an article of merchandise at the highest practicable profit, and the other is interested in obtaining it at the lowest possible price. Of the small, cunning lies that pass back and forth over that counter, of the half-truths told, and the whole truths suppressed, of deceptions touching the quality of goods on one side and the ability to buy on the other, it would be humiliating to tell. If every lie told in the shops, across mahogany and show-case, by buyers and sellers, were nailed like base coin to the counter, there would be no room for the display of goods. It is considered no mean compliment to a business man to say that he is sharp at a bargain; yet this sharpness is rarely more than the faculty of ingenious lying. A man who sells to me an article worth only five dollars for twice that sum is a "a sharp man;" but he cannot make such a sale to me without telling me, in some way, a lie. The price he puts upon his merchandise is a lie, essentially, in itself.

There is a great deal of business lying that by long habit becomes unconscious. If we take up a newspaper, we shall find that quite a number of the stores around us, kept by our excellent friends, have "the largest and finest stock of goods ever displayed in the city." We shall find that they have been selling for years at "unprecedentedly low prices," that they are "selling at less than cost," that they are pushing off goods at rates "ruinously low," and that they can offer bargains to buyers that will confound their competitors. I suppose that none of these advertisers think they are lying, or, if they do, that their lying is of a harmful character. Lying in this way is supposed to be part of the legitimate machinery of trade. Promising definitely to finish work without the expectation of keeping the promise, or being able to keep it, is another kind of half unconscious lying. There are men engaged in various trades, in all communities, whose word is of no more value, when in the form of a promise to finish within a certain period a certain piece of work, than the fly-leaf of a last year's almanac. There are men whom every one knows who will lie without blushing about their work, and who will stand at their counter and lie all day, and then sleep with a peaceful conscience at night, having failed to fulfil a single pledge during their waking hours. Then there are people who will promise to pay bills, and promise a hundred times over, and never pay, and never expect to pay. When a bill is presented, they promise to pay, as a matter of course; and that is considered as good as the gold, until it is presented again; and then comes another promise, and another and another. The creditor knows the debtor lies, but many a debtor of this kind would feel insulted and injured by any spoken doubts of his truthfulness.

But the field is large, and I am already beyond the limits which I set for myself in these essays. It will be seen that I regard truthfulness as, on the whole, a rare article in this world. It is in some respects necessarily so. Many men are incapable of stating a fact or telling a truth. They have not the power to comprehend or express either. The majority of men receive truth through such media of prejudice, selfishness, bigotry, sensuality, and the like, that they never get it pure, and are therefore incapable of uttering it correctly, even when their power of expression equals their power of perception, which is not commonly the case. So there is a world of unconscious lying; but I am sorry to believe that there is just as large a world of conscious lying. In politics, society, and business, the conscious and intentional lie abounds. "Lord! how this world is given to lying!"

Well, all this can be improved. Men can cultivate the power to apprehend and express truth. They can cast off the prejudice, selfishness, bigotry, and sensuality that prevent them from receiving truth. They can refrain from conscious lying; and no one doubts that the world would be greatly improved by honest efforts directed to these ends. Only the naked soul, in Eternity's white light, can be wholly truthful; but we can all try for it, and we shall find our highest account in trying.

LESSON VI.

MISTAKES OF PENANCE.

"For of the soul the body form doth take,
For soul is form and doth the body make."

SPENSER.

"Can sackcloth clothe a fault or hide a shame?
Or do thy hands make Heaven a recompense,
By strewing dust upon thy briny face?
No! though thou pine thyself with willing want,
Or face look thin, or carcass ne'er so gaunt;
Such holy madness God rejects and loathes
That sinks no deeper than the skin or clothes."

QUARLES.

"Beauty is truth, truth beauty."

KEATS.

I HAVE every reason to believe that God loves Shakers, but I do not think He admires them. I do not see how He can; but perhaps this is not a competent reason to offer in the premises. I saw a wagon-load of what I supposed to be Shakers of both sexes, riding along the street, the other day; and I wondered what I should think of them if I had made them. I think I should have been about equally vexed and amused to see the lines that I had made beautiful, disguised, and every grace-giving swell of limb and bust, upon which I had exercised such exquisite toil, carefully hidden. They sat up very straight and prim, in a very square wagon, behind a square-trotting horse, driven by "right lines" in a pair of hands that seemed to grow out of the driver's stomach, while his elevated, rectangular elbows cut rigidly against the air on either side. It was a vision for a painter—a house painter—"a painter by trade." The long-haired, meek-looking men, with their flat-crowned, broad-brimmed hats, straight coats and neutral colors, and the women with their sugar-scoop bonnets, white kerchiefs and straight waists, looked like a case of faded wax-figures, in prison uniform, that had "come down to us from a former generation."

I heaved a sigh as the wagon-load of mortified and badly-dressed flesh passed out of sight, and wondered if the souls inside of those bodies were as angular as their covering. I did not believe it—I do not believe it. I have no doubt that underneath those straight waistcoats hearts have throbbed at the sight of woman and child, and longed for home and family life, with yearnings that could not be uttered. Those straight-laced sensibilities have been thrilled by beauty, and bathed in the grace and glory of the life around them.

Trees have whispered to them, flowers have looked up and rebuked them, brooks have called to them with laughter, rivers have smiled upon them in sunshine, the great sky has bent over them with infinite tenderness and fulness of beauty, and they have felt what they could not define. It was something very wrong, they supposed, and so they buttoned their straight jackets around them, turned their eyes away from beholding vanity, and thought they had done an excellent thing. I know that those young women, with their abominable clothing outside, and their crushed and abused sympathies inside, are unhappy, unless they have all been mercifully transformed into fanatics. It is useless to tell me that a man can ignore or trample to death the strongest passion of his nature—the strongest, the purest, and the most ennobling—and be a happy man. It is useless to say that a man or woman can walk through a world of beauty—themselves the most beautiful of all things—and bind themselves up in unbecoming drapery, and smother all their impulses to express the beauty with which God inspires them, and do it with content and satisfaction. It cannot be done.

So, when this wagon-load of Shakers drove out of sight, I heaved a sigh, for I knew that not to be unhappy in the life which was typefied in their dress and establishment, would be a greater misfortune, essentially, than dissatisfaction and discontent would be. If they were happy in their life, they must have become perverted in their natures, or indurated beyond the susceptibility to receive the impressions of healthy men and women. If God ever put any thing majestic and noble into a man, and gave him a fitting frame for it, He never intended that it should be hidden in a meal-bag, or permanently quenched under a smock-frock. In the infinite variety which he has introduced into human character and into human forms and faces, there is no warrant for dressing men in uniform, but a most emphatic protest against it. If God made woman beautiful, He made her so to be looked at—to give pleasure to the eyes which rest upon her—and she has no business to dress herself as if she were a hitching-post, or to transform that which should give delight to those among whom she moves, into a ludicrous caricature of a woman's form.

I repeat that I have every reason to believe that God loves Shakers, but I do not think He admires them. If God admires the bodies He has made, He cannot admire them when they are covered by the Shaker dress, for it spoils the looks of them, and differs essentially from the plan which He pursues in draping all other forms of life. There is no grace about it, and no beauty of color. God admires clouds, I doubt not, when painted by the setting sun, and stars flashing in the heavens, and the flowers of myriad hues that are scattered over the earth, but if these are objects of His special admiration, as they are of ours, what can He think of a drab Shaker bonnet? What can He think when man and woman, the glory and crown of His creation, are entirely overtopped and thrown into the shade by birds and bees and blossoms, and go poking around the world in unexampled and ingeniously contrived ugliness? What does He think of men and women who take that passion of love, which was intended to make them happy, and give them sweet companionship, and bear young children to their arms, and trample it under their feet as an unholy thing, and to welcome to their hearts, in its stead, blackness, and darkness, and tempest? What does He think of lives out of which are shut all meaning and all individuality, and all love and expression of beauty, and all vivifying, liberalizing, and humanizing experience?

I owe no grudge to the Shakers. I like their apple-sauce, (they ask a thrifty price for it,) and have faith in the genuineness and the generation, under favorable conditions, of their garden seeds; but I object to their style of life and piety, and to every thing outside of Shakerdom which looks like it. I object to this whole idea, (and the Shakers have not monopolized it,) that God takes delight in the voluntary personal mortification of His children, and that He approves of their going about, sad-faced and straight-laced, studiously avoiding all temptation to enjoy themselves.

I have seen a deacon in the pride of his deep humility. He combed his hair straight, and looked studiously after the main chance; and while he looked, he employed himself in setting a good example. His dress was rigidly plain, and his wife was not indulged in the vanities of millinery and mantua-making. He never joked. He did not know what a joke was, any further than to know that it was a sin. He carried a Sunday face through the week. He did not mingle in the happy social parties of his neighborhood. He was a deacon. He starved his social nature because he was a deacon. He refrained from all participation in a free and generous life because he was a deacon. He made his children hate Sunday because he was a deacon. He so brought them up that they learned to consider themselves unfortunate in being the children of a deacon. They were pitied by other children because they were the children of a deacon. His wife was pitied by other women because she was the wife of a deacon. Nobody loved him. If he came into a circle where men were laughing or telling stories, they always stopped until he went out. Nobody ever grasped his hand cordially, or slapped him on the shoulder, or spoke of him as a good fellow. He seemed as dry and hard and tough as a piece of jerked beef. There was no softness of character—no juiciness—no loveliness in him.

Now it is of no use for me to undertake to realize to myself that God admires such a character as this. I do not doubt that He loves the man, as He loves all men; but to admire his style of manhood and piety is impossible for any intelligent being. It lacks the roundness and fulness, and richness and sweetness, that belong to a truly admirable character. Such a man caricatures Christianity, and scares other men away from it. Such a man ostentatiously presents himself as one in whose life religion is dominant. It is religion that is supposed to rub down that long face, and inspire that stiff demeanor, and to make him at all points an unattractive and unlovable man. Of course it is not religion that does any thing of the kind, but it has the credit of it with the world, and the world does not like it. It looks around, and sees a great many men who do not pretend to religion at all, and yet who are very lovable men. If religion can transform a pleasant man into a most unpleasant one, and change a free, bright, and happy home into a dismal place of slavery, and blot out a man's æsthetic and social nature, the world naturally thinks that getting religion would be almost as much of a misfortune as getting some melancholy chronic disease, and I do not blame it. It is not to be wondered at that the world should mistake, very much, the true nature of Christianity, when Christians themselves entertain such grievous errors about it.

I suppose God is attracted to very much the same style of character that men are. Christ loved a young man at first sight, who lacked the very thing essential to his highest manhood. But He loved the kind of man He saw before Him. He was upright, frank-hearted, open-minded, and bright; and "Jesus beholding him, loved him." There are men whom one cannot help loving and admiring though they lack a great many things—things very "needful" to make them perfect men. Now I put it to good, conscientious, Christian men and women, whether they do not take more pleasure in the society of a warm-hearted, generous, chivalrous, well-fed, man of the world, than in the society of any of that class of Christians of whom the deacon I have mentioned is a type. I know they do, and they cannot help it. There is more of that which belongs to a first-class Christian character in the former than in the latter, and if I were called upon to test the two men by commanding them respectively to sell what they have and give to the poor, I should be disappointed were the deacon to behave the best. A character which religion does not fructify—does not soften, enlarge, beautify, and enrich—is not benefited by religion—or, rather, has not possessed itself of religion. God loves that which is beautiful and attractive in character, just as much as we do, and it makes no difference where he sees it. He does not dislike the amiable traits of a sinner because he is a sinner, nor does he admire those traits of a Christian which we feel to be contemptible, simply because they belong to a Christian. A Christian sucked dry of his humanity, is as juiceless and as flavorless as a sucked orange, and I believe that God regards him in the same light that we do. He will save such I doubt not, for their faith; and, in the coming world, they will learn what they do not know here; but the question whether they are as well worth saving as some of their neighbors, may, I think, be legitimately entertained. In saying this, I mean to be neither light or irreverent. I mean simply to indicate that some men are worth a great deal more to themselves and to their fellows than others.

So, when I look abroad upon the world, and see men shaving their heads, and wearing nasty hair shirts, and shutting themselves up in cells, and living lives of celibacy, and when I see women retiring from the world which they were sent to adorn, populate, and bless, and Shakers driving around in square wagons and studiously ugly garments, and Christians who should know better abandoning all the bright and cheerful things of life, and feeling that there is merit in mortification, I cannot but feel that God looks down upon it all with sadness and pity. After doing every thing in His power to make His children happy—after filling the world with good things for their use, and giving them abundant faculties for enjoying them—after endowing them with beauty, and a sense of that which is beautiful—it must be sad to Him to see them wandering about in strange disguises, hugging to their half-rebellious hearts the awful mistake that, however much they may suffer, they are gaining favor thereby in the sight of their Maker. Of course, I believe in self-denial, and in the nobility of self-denial, for the good of others; but I believe that all self-denial that partakes of the character of penance, in whatever form and under whatever circumstances it may develop itself, is always a thing of mischief, and always a thing of error. It has its basis in the miserable theory that there is something in the passions and appetites with which God has constituted man that is essentially bad—a theory as impious as it is injurious—as fatal to all just conceptions of the divine Being and of man's relations to Him, as to all human happiness.

Every thing which is truly admirable is good, and good and desirable in the degree by which it is admirable. A beautiful face and form are admirable, and just as good as they are admirable—just as good in their element of beauty. They are good for that quality, and in that quality, which excites our admiration. A beautiful bonnet, a beautiful dress, a beautiful brooch or necklace, are all admirable, and good because they are admirable, or good because every thing admirable is necessarily good. A family over which the father presides with tender dignity, and in which the mother moves with love's divinest ministry—where the faces of innocent children are shining, while their voices make music sweeter than the morning songs of birds—is admirable, and it is good in all those respects which make it admirable. A well-dressed man or woman is admirable, and that thing is good in itself which makes them so. A man who carries his heart in his hand, who deals both justly and generously by men, who bears a sunny face and pleasant words into society, whose cultured mind enriches freely all with whom it is brought into relation, who has abundant charity for the weak and erring, and who takes life and what it brings him contentedly, is an admirable man, and good in all the points which make him admirable. A house that presents a harmonious and handsome interior to the eye of the passenger, and whose exterior combines equal convenience and elegance, is admirable, and, by that token, good.

Now these very simple propositions have their correlatives, which it is not necessary to set down in order, any further than fairly to illustrate my point. Things that are not admirable are not good. If the dress of a Shaker is not admirable, it is not good. If that sort of life which is led in a cloister, by monks or nuns, is not admirable, it is not good. If a man who professes to be a Christian lives a life out of which is shut all with which an unsophisticated humanity sympathizes—a life barren of attractive fruit—a life bare in all its surroundings—a life with no genial outflow and expression—a life of niggardly negatives rather than of generous positives—then that life is not admirable, and if it be not admirable it cannot be good in those respects. A man may carry along with such a life as this a spotless conscience and a strict devotion to apprehended duty, and these may be admirable and good, but the other characteristics cannot be either; and however much God may approve his honest heart and honest endeavor, He cannot admire the style of manhood in which they have their dull and difficult illustration. The idea that I wish definitely to convey is this: that on the basis of a right heart, God would have us build up a bright, generous, genial, expressive Christian character, and use gratefully and gladly all those things which He has prepared to make life cheerful and admirable. I believe a saint ought to have a better tailor than a sinner, and be in all manly ways a better fellow. I believe a true Christian should be in every thing that constitutes and belongs to a man the most admirable man in the world.

I have an idea that God looks with the same kind

of contempt on the prominent characteristics of certain styles of Christian men and women, that men of the world do. There is nothing admirable in cant and whine, and nasal psalm-singing, and men whose hearts are livers and whose blood is bile; and I cannot believe that He blames people for not admiring them, and not being attracted to them. I do not believe that an admirable Christian life is repulsive to the men of the world. I believe that wherever the human mind recognizes a rounded, chastened, rich, and outspoken Christian character, whether it belong to manhood or womanhood, it admires it, and feels attracted to it, by the degree in which it admires it. I believe, moreover, that the Christianity which discards as vanities those things which God has provided for the pleasure of His children, and mortifies the love of beauty, and adopts the theory that God is pleased with penance, and degrades, abuses, and traduces the body to win greater sanctity of soul, and finds a sin in every sweet of sense, is a bastard Christianity. God is not the God of the dead, but of the living.

LESSON VII.

THE RIGHTS OF WOMAN.

"Heard melodies are sweet, but those unheard
Are sweeter; therefore ye soft pipes play on;
Not to the sensual ear, but, more endeared,
Pipe to the spirit ditties of no tones."

JOHN KEATS.

"I am as free as Nature first made man."

DRYDEN.

"What she wills to do or say
Seems wisest, virtuousest, discreetest, best."

MILTON.

IT was the sarcastic remark of a crusty old parson of Connecticut that woman has the undoubted right to shave and sing bass, if she chooses to do so. I question the right of bearded man to shave himself, and I will not concede that woman has a superior right, based on inferior necessities; but believing that man has an undoubted right to sing bass, I am inclined to accord the same right to woman. Woman is a female man, and there is no reason that I know of why she should not have the same rights, precisely, that a male man has. I claim for myself, and for man, the privilege of singing treble, under certain circumstances; and why should I not accord to woman the right to sing bass? The brave old chorals of Germany would hardly be sung with much effect were the airs denied to the masculine voice, yet if it be man's prerogative to sing bass, it is surely woman's to sing treble. If it be usurpation for her to grope among the gutturals of the masculine clef, it is gross presumption for him to attempt to leap the five-rail fence that stands between him and high C. I put this consideration forward for the purpose of stopping every caviller's mouth upon the subject, until I present arguments of a broader and more comprehensive character, in support of woman's right to sing bass.

It is claimed by those who deny woman's right to sing bass that she is needed for the treble and alto parts. Needed by whom? Needed by man? But who gave man the right to set up his needs as the law of woman's life? If man needs treble and alto, I hope he may get them. He has the undoubted right to sing both parts to suit his own fancy, or to hire others to do it for him. Man needs buttons on his shirts, and clean linen, but for the life of me I cannot see why that need defines a woman's duty in any respect. Let him do his own washing, and sew on his own buttons. Suppose a woman should need to have hooks and eyes sewed upon her dress, as some of them do, sometimes, after taking a very long breath, would that determine it to be man's duty to sew them on? "It is a poor rule that will not work both ways." This is one of the illustrations of man's selfishness—that he sets up his needs as the rule by which the rights of one-half of the human race are to be determined.

This same selfishness of man will demand that I reconsider this talk, and will accuse me of sophistry. It will declare that I do not state the case fairly. It will say that woman needs money with which to buy her dresses and procure her food, and strong hands to labor for her and protect her, and that these needs do indeed define man's duty with respect to her. But I place all this on the ground of gallantry and humanity. Of course, we are all very glad to do these things, you know,—we who have human feelings—but woman has no right to them, based upon her need—particularly if she be a woman who insists, as I do, upon her indefeasible right to sing bass. I know that it helps things along for a woman to look after a man's linen and buttons, and do his fine work generally, because she seems to have a kind of natural knack at the business. I am aware that it is exceedingly pleasant to hear a woman sing treble, if she sings it well, but I am talking, be it remembered, of woman's right to sing bass. Let us stick to the question.

The enemies of this highest among the rights of woman are fond of alluding to the fact that only here and there a woman can be found who wishes to avail herself of her right, and practically to enter upon the work of singing bass. The large majority of women prefer to sing the soprano, while a few, of moderate views, adopt alto as a kind of compromise. But what has this fact to do with the matter of right in the premises? Most people prefer beef-steak without onions, but I never knew that fact to be brought forward as an argument against the right of a man to eat it with onions. It is possible, indeed, that if people were more accustomed to eating beef-steak with onions, or those savory vegetables were less objectionable in their style of perfume, there would be a majority in favor of the associated luxuries. We must remember, too, in considering this aspect of the question, that woman is, to a certain extent, a creature of whims. She is exceedingly apt to adopt a practice because it is fashionable. If it were fashionable for woman to sing bass, how long would it be before the lower tones would find full development? And how long would it be before the men themselves would repeat those words of the immortal bard:—

"Her voice was ever soft,
Gentle and *low*,—An excellent thing in woman"?

After all, this sort of argument against woman's right to sing bass answers itself. If the preference of women generally for the soprano and alto be a good reason for their confining themselves to the performance of those parts, then a change of preference would be a valid reason for their leaving them. If individual right goes with general preference, then the pillars of the universe are uprooted, or we have no pillars worth mentioning. I suppose that women generally prefer in-door to out-of-door employments—labor that draws less upon muscle, and more upon ingenuity and delicate-fingered facility; but that settles nothing as to their right to engage in muscular toils in the open air. The German peasant-woman has labored out-of-doors for many generations. The result has been the gradual approach to each other of her hips and shoulders, the extinguishment of that portion of her person known as the waist, and some noticeable flatness over the cerebral organs; but the German peasant-woman has her right, and that is worth any sacrifice, you know. If she prefers hoeing cabbages to spinning flax, who shall hinder her? If all women should prefer hoeing cabbages to spinning flax, or any variety of yarn, who shall hinder them? So far as man is concerned, woman has a right to grow her shoulders just as near her hips, and wear a head as flat as she pleases. In short, the general preference of women with respect to any thing decides no question of individual right, whatever.

I will not admit that the general preference of women for private life imposes any obligation upon any woman to abstain from public life, or affects in any way her right to enter upon public life. I am aware that one would not like to have one's wife or sister an opera-singer, or a public dancer, or a preacher, or a doctor in general practice, or a circus-rider, or a popular lecturer, or an actress; but I am talking about the question of right. Most women would shrink from war—from its fatigues, its dangers, its bloody strife; but Joan of Arc asserted her right to go into war; and her name is engrossed upon the scroll of fame. All women have the same right to go to war that she had. I confess that I should like to see a regiment of women six feet high, officered by women, all dressed in Balmorals illustrating the national colors, marching to battle in as close order as the peculiarity of their garments would permit, and accompanied by a corps of cavalry in side-saddles. Such an assertion of woman's right would be grand beyond description. I should not care to live on very intimate terms with the colonel of the regiment, but I don't know as that has any thing to do with this question.

I was talking, however, about the right of women to sing bass, and must go on. It is declared by those who oppose this right that woman has no natural organs and aptitudes for bass. This is the strong-point of the enemy, but it amounts to nothing. If woman fails, apparently, in organs and aptitudes for this part, it only shows what long years of abuse will accomplish. Let us never forget in this discussion that woman is only a female man, that there is no such thing as "sex of soul," and that woman's vocal organs are built exactly like man's—as much like man's as her hands and her feet and her head are like his—a little smaller, perhaps, —that's all. It is a familiar fact, I presume, that the little colts born of South American dams take to ambling as their natural step, simply because the men of South America have taught the fathers and mothers of these colts to amble through uncounted generations. Now in North America we train horses to trot, and the consequence is that amblers are scarce, and in most cases have to be educated to their gait. This is the way in which nature adapts herself to popular want and popular usage. The large variety of apples which load our orchards were developed from the insignificant crab, and the peach was the child of the almond, or the almond of the peach—I have forgotten which. Now I suppose (with some feeble doubts about it) that man and woman started exactly together, that her singing treble better than she does bass results from usage, and that her singing treble rather than bass was purely a matter of accident at first. All analogy teaches me that if she had begun on bass, and the other part had been given to man, we should be hearing to-day of Ma'lle Patti, "the charming new baritone," and "the magnificent basso," Madame Jenny Lind Goldschmidt, while admiring crowds would toss flowers to Carl Formes, "the unapproachable soprano," or Mario, "the king of contraltos."

I suppose that those who maintain that woman has no natural organs and aptitudes for singing bass, would say that she has no natural organs and aptitudes for boxing and playing at ball. Just because woman holds her fists the wrong side up, as if she were kneading bread rather than flesh, it is claimed that she was not made for the "manly art of self-defence," and from the wholly incompetent facts that she cannot throw a ball three feet against a common north-west wind, and is not as fleet as a deer, it is judged that she has no right to engage in base-ball. But suppose all women had been accustomed to boxing and playing ball as much as the men have been; would they not have arrived at corresponding excellence? I know that as women are now (and they please me exceedingly) they have not muscle to "hit from the shoulder" with force sufficient to make them formidable antagonists; and I am aware that they lack something in the length of limb requisite for the rapid locomotion of the ball-ground;

but they have never had a chance. See what the washerwomen have done for themselves. They seem to be a separate race of beings, for they all have large arms, and shoulders that would do honor to Tom Sayers. I have seen negro slave women at work in the field, with a muscular development that would be the envy of a Bowery boy. The washerwoman and the field slave show what can be done by cultivation. I know that their style of figure is not quite so attractive as I have seen, and I know that wherever there is an extraordinary tax upon muscle there is an extraordinary repression of mind and blunting of the sensibilities, but it must be remembered that we are talking about rights, now. I claim and maintain, (I may as well come out with the whole of it,) that a woman has a right to do any thing she chooses to do, with perhaps the unimportant exception of becoming the father of a family.

The truth is that women have never had a fair chance. They can do any thing they are trained to do. The proper physical culture of woman, carried on through a competent number of generations, would develop her beyond all our present conceptions. She would be likely to arrive at a high condition of muscle and a low condition of mind, very unlike our present idea of the noblest type of womanhood; but very possibly our ideals of womanhood are conventional, or traditional. She has hands, and has a right to use them; a tongue, and the right to wag it in her own way; powers corresponding to those of man in all important respects, and the right to develop and employ them according to her taste and choice. I deny, to man, the privilege of defining the rights and duties of woman. A woman is mistress of her own actions and judge of her own powers and aptitudes; and if any woman thinks that she can do a man's work better than what society considers her own, then she has an undeniable right to do it, if she can get it to do, and is willing to accept the work with the conditions that attend it.

I am a firm believer in "woman's rights"—especially her right to do as she pleases. It is possible that, before the law, she is not in possession of all her rights, but all wrongs in this direction will be corrected as time progresses. I speak particularly at this time of her right to sing bass, because it is a representative right, and covers, as with a lid, a whole chest full of others. Yet while I claim this right, I confess that I should not care to see it exercised to any great extent, for I think that treble is, by all odds, the finer and more attractive part in music. Is it worth while to exercise the right of singing bass, when it costs a good deal to get up a voice for it, and when treble comes natural and easy, and is very much pleasanter to the ear? Bass would be a bad thing for a lullaby, and could only silence a baby by scaring it. If I should have committed to me the melodies of the world, I would care very little about my right to sing those subordinate parts that gather around them in obedient harmonies. At least, I think I would, unless some upstart man should deny my right to sing any thing but melodies. If it were committed to me to sing like a bird, I would not care, I think, to exercise my right to roar like a bull. If I can witch the ears and win the hearts of men and women by doing that which I can do easily and naturally and well, then I shall do best not to exercise my right to do that which I can only do difficultly, and unnaturally, and ill.

Woman, in my apprehension, is the mistress, not alone of the melody of music, but of the melody of life. Whatever it may be possible to do by cultivation and a long course of development, it is doubtful whether a woman would ever sing bass well. I am aware that she has the right, and the organs, but I question whether her bass would amount to any thing—whether it would be worth singing. When women talk with me about their right to vote, and their right to practise law, and their right to engage in any business which usage has assigned to man, I say "yes—you have all those rights." I never dispute with them at all. Indeed, you see how I have put myself forward as the defender of these same rights; yet I should be sorry to see them exercised by the women I admire and love. It is all very well to say that the presence of woman at the ballot-box would purify it, and restrain the manners of the men around it; but I have seen enough of the world to learn that all human influence is reciprocal and reactionary. Man and the ballot-box might gain, but woman would lose, and men and the ballot-box themselves would lose in the long run. The ballot-box is the bass, and it should be man's business to sing it, while woman should give him home melody with which it should harmonize.

In the matter of rights, I suppose that I should not differ materially with any strong-minded woman; but I have always observed that the most truly lovable, humble, pure-hearted, God-fearing and humanity-loving women of my acquaintance, never say any thing about these rights, and scorn those of their sex who do. I have never known a woman who was at once satisfied in her affections and discontented with her woman's lot and her woman's work. There is a weak place, or a wrong place, or a rotten place, in the character or nature of every woman who stands and howls upon the spot where her Creator placed her, and neglects her own true work and life while claiming the right to do the work and live the life of man. I will admit all the rights that such a woman claims—all that I myself possess—if she will let me alone, and keep her distance from me. She may sing bass, but I do not wish to hear her. She is repulsive to me. She offends me.

I believe in women. I believe they are the sweetest, purest, most unselfish, best part of the human race. I have no doubt on this subject, whatever. They do sing the melody in all human life, as well as the melody in music. They carry the leading part, at least in the sense that they are a step in advance of us, all the way in the journey heavenward. I believe that they cannot move very widely out of the sphere which they now occupy, and remain as good as they now are; and I deny that my belief rests upon any sentimentality, or jealousy, or any other weak or unworthy basis. A man who has experienced a mother's devotion, a wife's self-sacrificing love, and a daughter's affection, and is grateful for all, may be weakly sentimental about some things, but not about women. He would help every woman he loves to the exercise of all the rights which hold dignity and happiness for her. He would fight that she might have those rights, if necessary; but he would rather have her lose her voice entirely, than to hear her sound a bass note so long as a demi-semi-quaver.

LESSON VIII.

AMERICAN PUBLIC EDUCATION.

"Keen are the pangs
Advancement often brings. To be secure,
Be humble. To be happy, be content."
JAMES HURDIS.

"For not that which men covet most is best;
Nor that thing worst which men do most refuse.
But fittest is that each contented rest
With that they hold." SPENSER.

"Men have different spheres. It is for some to evolve great moral truths, as the Heavens evolve stars, to guide the sailor on the sea and the traveller on the desert; and it is for some, like the sailor and the traveller, simply to be guided."—BEECHER.

A VENERABLE gentleman who once occupied a prominent position in a leading New England college, was remarking recently upon the difficulty which he experienced in obtaining servants who would attend to their duties. He had just dismissed a girl of sixteen, who was so much "above her business" as to be intolerable. The girl's father, who was an Englishman, called upon him for an explanation. The employer told his story, every word of which the father received without question, and then remarked, with considerable vehemence: "*It is all owing to those cursed public schools.*" The father retired, and the old professor sat down and thought about it; and the result of his thinking did not differ materially from that of the father. It was not, of course, that there was any thing in the studies pursued which had tended to unfit the girl for her duties. It was very possible indeed for the girl to have been a better servant in consequence of her intelligence. There was nothing in English grammar or the multiplication table to produce insubordination and discontent. There was nothing in the whole case that tended to condemn public schools, as such; but it was the spirit inculcated by the teachers of public schools, which had spoiled this girl for her place, and which has spoiled, and is still spoiling, thousands of others.

Let us look for a moment into the influence of such a motto as the following, written over a school-house door—always before the eyes of the pupils, and always alluded to by school committees and visitors who are invited to "make a few remarks":

"*Nothing is impossible to him who wills.*"

This abominable lie is placed before a room full of children and youth, of widely varying capacities, and great diversity of circumstances. They are called upon to look at it, and believe in it. Suppose a girl of humble mental abilities and humble circumstances looks at this motto, and says: "I 'will' be a lady. I 'will' be independent. I 'will' be subject to no man's or woman's bidding." Under these circumstances, the girl's father, who is poor, removes her from school, and tells her that she must earn her living. Now I ask what kind of a spirit she can carry into her service, except that of surly and impudent discontent? She has been associating in school, perhaps, with girls whom she is to serve in the family she enters. Has she not been made unfit for her place by the influences of the public school? Have not her comfort and her happiness been spoiled by those influences? Is her reluctant service of any value to those who pay her the wages of her labor?

It is safe, at least, to make the proposition that public schools are a curse to all the youth whom they unfit for their proper places in the world. It is the favorite theory of teachers that every man can make of himself any thing that he really chooses to make. They resort to this theory to rouse the ambition of their more sluggish pupils, and thus get more study out of them. I have known entire schools instructed to aim at the highest places in society, and the most exalted offices of life. I have known enthusiastic old fools who made it their principal business to go from school to school, and talk such stuff to the pupils as would tend to unfit every one of humble circumstances and slender possibilities for the life that lay before him. The fact is persistently ignored, in many of these schools, established emphatically for the education of the people, that the majority of the places in this world are subordinate and low places. Every boy and girl is taught to "be something" in the world, which would be very well if being "something" were being what God intended they should be; but when being "something" involves the transformation of what God intended should be a respectable shoemaker into a very indifferent and a very slow minister of the Gospel, the harmful and even the ridiculous character of the instruction becomes apparent.

There are two classes of evil results attending the inculcation of these favorite doctrines of the school teachers—first, the unfitting of men and women for humble places; and, second, the impulsion of men of feeble power into high places, for the duties of which they have neither natural nor acquired fitness. There are no longer any American girls who go out to service in families. They went into mills from the chamber and the kitchen, but now they have left the mills, and their places are filled by Scotch and Irish girls. Why is this? Is it because that among the American girls there are none of poverty, and of humble powers? Is it because they are not wanted? Or is it because they have become unfitted for such services as these, and feel above them? Is it not because they have become possessed of notions that would render them uncomfortable in family service, and render any family they might serve uncomfortable? An American servant, who good-naturedly accepts her condition, and knows and loves her place, who is willing to acknowledge that she has a mistress, and who enters into her department of the family life as a harmonious and happy member, may exist, but I do not know her. People have ceased inquiring for American servants. They would like them, generally, because they are intelligent and Protestant, but they cannot get them because they are unwilling to accept service, and the obligations and conditions it imposes. Where all the American girls are, I do not know. I can remember the time when thrifty farmers, mechanics, and tradesmen took wives from the kitchens of gentlemen where they were employed,—good, intelligent, self-respectful women they were, too—who became modest mistresses of thrifty families afterward;—but that is all done with now. Under the present mode of education, nobody is fitted for a low place, and everybody is taught to look for a high one.

If we go into a school exhibition, our ears are deafened by declamation addressed to ambition. The boys have sought out from literature every stirring appeal to effort, and every extravagant promise of reward. The compositions of the girls are of the same general tone. We hear of "infinite yearnings," from the lips of girls who do not know enough to make a pudding, and of being polished "after the similitude of a palace" from those who do not comprehend the commonest duties of life. Every thing is on the high-pressure principle. The boys, all of them, have the general idea that every thing that is necessary to become great men is to try for it; and each one supposes it possible for him to become Governor of the State, or President of the Union. The idea of being educated to fill a humble office in life is hardly thought of, and every bumpkin who has a memory sufficient for the words repeats the stanza:—

"Lives of great men all remind us
We can make our lives sublime,
And departing, leave behind us
Footprints on the sands of time."

There is a fine ring to this familiar quatrain of Mr. Longfellow, but it is nothing more than a musical cheat. It sounds like truth, but it is a lie. The lives of great men all remind us that they have made their own memory sublime, but they do not assure us at all that we can leave footprints like theirs behind us. If you do not believe it, go to the cemetery yonder.

There they lie—ten thousand upturned faces—ten thousand breathless bosoms. There was a time when fire flashed in those vacant orbits, and warm ambitions pulsed in those bosoms. Dreams of fame and power once haunted those hollows skulls. Those little piles of bones that once were feet ran swiftly and determinedly through forty, fifty, sixty, seventy years of life; but where are the prints they left? "He lived—he died—he was buried"—is all that the headstone tells us. We move among the monuments, we see the sculpture, but no voice comes to us to say that the sleepers are remembered for any thing they ever did. Natural affection pays its tribute to its departed object, a generation passes by, the stone grows gray, and the man has ceased to be, and is to the world as if he had never lived. Why is it that no more have left a name behind them? Simply because they were not endowed by their Maker with the power to do it, and because the offices of life are mainly humble, requiring only humble powers for their fulfilment. The cemeteries of one hundred years hence will be like those of to-day. Of all those now in the schools of this country, dreaming of fame, not one in twenty thousand will be heard of then,—not one in twenty thousand will have left a footprint behind him.

Now I believe that a school, in order to be a good one, should be one that will fit men and women, in the best way, for the humble positions that the great mass of them must necessarily occupy in life. It is not necessary that boys and girls be taught any less than they are taught now. They should receive more practical knowledge than they do now, without a doubt, and less of that which is simply ornamental, but they cannot know too much. An intelligent gardener is better than a clod-hopper, and an educated nurse is better than an ignorant one; but if the gardener and the nurse have been spoiled for their business and their condition, by the sentiments which they have imbibed with their knowledge, they are made uncomfortable to themselves, and to those whom they serve. I do not care how much knowledge a man may have acquired in school, that school has been a curse to him if its influence has been to make him unhappy in his place, and to fill him with futile ambitions.

The country has great reason to lament the effect of the kind of instruction upon which I have remarked. The universal greed for office is nothing but an indication of the appetite for distinction which has been diligently fed from childhood. It is astonishing to see the rush for office on the occasion of the change of a State or National Administration. Men will leave quiet and remunerative employments, and subject themselves to mean humiliations, simply to get their names into a newspaper, and to achieve a little official importance and social distinction. This desire for distinction seems to run through the whole social body, as a kind of moral scrofula, developing itself in various ways, according to circumstances and peculiarities of constitution. The consequence is that politics have become the pursuit of small men, and we no longer have an opportunity to put the best men into office. The scramble for place among fools is so great and so successful, that men of dignity and modesty retire from the field in disgust. Everybody wants to "be something," and in order to be something, everbody must leave his proper place in the world, and assume a position which God never intended he should fill. Look in upon a State legislature once, and you will find sufficient illustration of my meaning. Not one man in five of the whole number possesses the first qualification for making the laws of a State, and half of them never read the constitution of the country. I mean no contempt for the good, honest men of whom our State legislatures are principally composed, but I wish simply to say that there is nothing in their quality of mind, habits of thought, intellectual power, or style of pursuits that fits them for the great and momentous functions of legislation. They are there, a set of "nobodies," mainly for the purpose of becoming "somebodies," and not for any object connected with the good of the State.

Somehow, all the students in all our schools get the

idea, that a man in order to be "somebody" must be in public life. Now think of the fact that the millions attending school in this country have in some way acquired this idea, and that only one in every one thousand of these is either needed in public life, or can win success there. Let this fact be realized, and it is easy to see that the nine hundred and ninety-nine will feel that they are somehow cheated out of their birthright. They desired to be in public life, and be "somebody," but they are not, and so their life grows tame and tasteless to them. They are disappointed. The men solace themselves with a petty justice's commission, or a town office of some kind, and the women—some of them—talk about "woman's rights," and make themselves notorious and ridiculous at public meetings. I think women have rights which they do not at present enjoy, but I have very little confidence in the motives of their petticoated champions, who court mobs, delight in notoriety, and glory in their opportunity to burst away from private life, and be recognized by the public as "somebodies." I insist on this:—that private and even obscure life is the normal condition of the great multitude of men and women in this world; and that, to serve this private life, public life is instituted. Public life has no legitimate significance save as it is related to the service of private life. It requires peculiar talents and peculiar education, and brings with it peculiar trials; and the man best fitted for it would be the last man confidently to assert his fitness for it.

Thousands seek to become "somebodies" through the avenues of professional life; and so professional life is full of "nobodies." The pulpit is crowded with goodish "nobodies"—men who have no power—no unction—no mission. They strain their brains to write common-places, and wear themselves out repeating the rant of their sect and the cant of their schools. The bar is cursed with "nobodies" as much as the pulpit. The lawyers are few; the pettifoggers are many. The bar, more than any other medium, is that through which the ambitious youth of the country seek to attain political eminence. Thousands go into the study of law, not so much for the sake of the profession, as for the sake of the advantages it is supposed to give them for political preferment. An ambitious boy who has taken it into his head to be "somebody," always studies law; and as soon as he is "admitted to the bar" he is ready to begin his political scheming. Multitudes of lawyers are a disgrace to their profession, and a curse to their country. They lack the brains necessary to make them respectable, and the morals requisite for good neighborhood. They live on quarrels, and breed them that they may live. They have spoiled themselves for private life, and they spoil the private life around them. As for the medical profession, I tremble to think how many enter it because they have neither piety enough for preaching, nor brains enough to practice law. When I think of the great army of little men that is yearly commissioned to go forth into the world with a case of sharp knives in one hand, and a magazine of drugs in the other, I heave a sigh for the human race. Especially is all this lamentable when we remember that it involves the spoiling of thousands of good farmers and mechanics, to make poor professional men, while those who would make good professional men are obliged to attend to the simple duties of life, and submit to preaching that neither feeds nor stimulates them, and medicine that kills or fails to cure them.

There must be something radically wrong in our educational system, when youth are generally unfitted for the station which they are to occupy, or are forced into professions for which they have no natural fitness. The truth is that the stuff talked to boys and girls alike, about "aiming high," and the assurances given them, indiscriminately, that they can be any thing that they choose to become, are essential nuisances. Our children all go to the public schools. They are all taught these things. They all go out into the world with high notions, and find it impossible to content themselves with their lot. They had hoped to realize in life that which had been promised them in school, but all their dreams have faded, and left them disappointed and unhappy. They envy those whom they have been taught to consider above them, and learn to count their own lives a failure. Girls starve in a mean poverty, or do worse, because they are too proud to work in a chamber, or go into a shop. American servants are obsolete, all common employments are at a discount, the professions are crowded to overflowing, the country throngs with demagogues, and a general discontent with a humble lot prevails, simply because the youth of America have had the idea drilled into them that to be in private life, in whatever condition, is to be, in some sense, a "nobody." It is possible that the schools are not exclusively to blame for this state of things, and that our political harangues, and even our political institutions, have something to do with it.

What we greatly need in this country is the inculcation of soberer views of life. Boys and girls are bred to discontent. Everybody is after a high place, and nearly everybody fails to get one; and, failing, loses heart, temper, and content. The multitude dress beyond their means, and live beyond their necessities, to keep up a show of being what they are not. Farmers' daughters do not love to become farmers' wives, and even their fathers and mothers stimulate their ambition to exchange their station for one which stands higher in the world's estimation. Humble employments are held in contempt, and humble powers are everywhere making high employments contemptible. Our children need to be educated to fill, in Christian humility, the subordinate offices of life which they must fill, and taught to respect humble callings, and to beautify and glorify them by lives of contented and glad industry. When public schools accomplish an end so desirable as this, they will fulfil their mission, and they will not before. I seriously doubt whether one school in a hundred, public or private, comprehends its duty in this particular. They fail to inculcate the idea that the majority of the offices of life are humble, that the powers of the majority of the youth which they contain have relation to those offices, that no man is respectable when he is out of his place, and that half of the unhappiness of the world grows out of the fact, that, from distorted views of life, men are in places where they do not belong. Let us have this thing altogether reformed.

LESSON IX.

PERVERSENESS.

"Because she's constant, he will change,
And kindest glances coldly meet,
And all the time he seems so strange,
His soul is fawning at her feet."
COVENTRY PATMORE.

"All that we seem to think of is to manage matters so as to do as little good and plague and disappoint as many people as possible."—HAZLITT.

IT seems to me, either that there is a great deal of human nature in a pig, or that there is a great deal of pig in human nature. I find myself always sympathizing with a pig that wishes to go in an opposite direction to that in which its owner would drive it. It would be a sufficient reason for me to desire to go eastward, that a man was behind me, with an oath in his mouth and a very heavy boot on his foot, endeavoring to drive me westward. We are jealous of our freedom. We naturally rise in opposition to a will that undertakes to command our movements. This is not the result of education at all; it is pure human nature. Command a child—who shall be only old enough to understand you—to refrain from some special act, and you excite in his heart a desire to do that act; and he will have, nine times in ten, no reason for his desire to do it but your command that he shall not. The youngest human soul that has a will at all, takes the first occasion to declare its independence.

Now, I believe this principle in human nature to be, in itself, good. It is that which declares a man's right to himself—that which asserts personal liberty in thought, will, and movement. I believe it existed in Adam and Eve, and that it is more than likely that the tree of the knowledge of good and evil was despoiled because our beautiful great-grandmother, (for whom I confess much sympathy and affection,) was forbidden to touch it. It is a principle which should always be carefully distinguished from perverseness, in all our dealings with young and old, and in all our estimates of human character. When a child obeys a man, or when one man obeys another, it should always be for good and sufficient reason. Neither child nor man should be expected to surrender his right to himself without the presentation to him of the proper motive. When, yielding to this motive, the soul consents to be directed or led, it becomes obedient. Compulsion may secure conformity, but never obedience. If I, as a child or man, am to yield myself to the direction of any other man, that man is bound to present to me an adequate motive for the surrender. God throws upon me personal responsibility—gives me to myself—and no man, parent or otherwise, can make me truly obedient without giving me the motive for obedience. When a child or a man fails to yield to the legitimate motives of obedience, he is perverse, and it is about perverseness in some of its forms of manifestation that I propose to talk in this article.

At starting, I must give perverseness a somewhat broader meaning than that thus far indicated. I will say that that person is perverse who, from vanity, or pride of opinion and will, or malice, or any mean consideration, refuses to yield his conduct and himself to those motives and influences which his reason and conscience recognize to be pure and good and true. In its least aggravated form, perhaps, we find it among lovers. Women will sometimes persistently ignore a passion which they know has taken full possession of them, and grieve the heart that loves them by a coldness and indifference which they do not feel at all. Rather than acknowledge their affection for one whose loss would kill them, or, what would be the same thing, kill the world for them, they have lied, grown sick, and gone nearly insane. This is a perverseness very uncommon. Sometimes lovers have been very tender and devoted so long as a doubt of ultimate mutual possession remained to give zest to their passion, but the moment this doubt has been removed, one or the other has become incomprehensibly indifferent.

I have noticed that very few married pairs are matches in the matter of warmth and expression of passion between the parties. The man will be all devotion and tenderness—brimming with expressions of affection and exhibitions of fondness, and the woman all coolness and passivity, or (which is much more common) the woman will be active in expression, lavishing caresses and tendernesses upon a man who very possibly grows harder and colder with every delicate proof that the whole wealth of his wife's nature is poured at his feet, as a libation upon an altar. It is here that we see some of the strangest cases of perverseness that it is possible to conceive. I know men who are not bad men—who, I suppose, really love and respect their wives—and who would deny themselves even to heroism to give them the comforts and luxuries of life, yet who find themselves moved to reject with poorly-covered scorn, and almost to resent, the varied expressions of affection to which those wives give utterance. I know wives who long to pour their hearts into the hearts of their husbands, and to get sympathetic and fitting response, but who are never allowed to do it. They live a constrained, suppressed, unsatisfied life. They absolutely pine for the privilege of saying freely what they feel, in all love's varied languages, toward men who love them, but who grow harder with every approach of tenderness and colder with every warm, invading breath. A shower that purifies the atmosphere, and refreshes the face of heaven itself, sours cream, just as love's sweetest expression sours these men.

I have known wives to walk through such an experience as this into a condition of abject slavery—to waste their affection without return, until they have become poor, and spiritless, and mean. I have known them to lose their will—to become the mere dependent mistresses of their husbands—to be creeping cravens in dwellings where it should be their privilege to move as radiant queens. I have known them thrown back upon themselves, until they have become bitter railers against their husbands—uncomfortable companions—openly and shamelessly flouting their affection. I do not know what to make of the perverseness which induces a man to repel the advances of a heart which worships him, and to become hard and tyrannical in the degree by which that heart seeks to express its affection for him. There are husbands who would take the declaration that they do not love their wives as an insult, yet who hold the woman who loves them in fear and restraint through their whole life. I know wives who move about their houses with a trembling regard to the moods and notions of their husbands—wives who have no more liberty than slaves, who never spend a cent of money without a feeling of guilt, and who never give an order about the house without the same doubt of their authority that they would have if they were only housekeepers, employed at a very economical salary. I can think of no proper punishment for such husbands except daily ducking in a horse-pond, until reformation. Yet these asses are so unconscious of their detestable habits of feeling and life, that, probably, not one of them who reads this will think that I mean him, but will wonder where I have lived to fall in with such outlandish people.

The most precious possession that ever comes to a man in this world is a woman's heart. Why some graceful and most amiable women whom I know will persist in loving some men whom I also know, is more than I know. I will not call their love an exhibition of perverseness, though it looks like it; but that these men with these rich, sweet hearts in their hands, grow sour and snappish, and surly and tyrannical and exacting, is the most unaccountable thing in the world. If a pig will not allow himself to be driven, he will follow a man who offers him corn, and he will eat the corn, even though he puts his feet in the trough ; but there are men—some of them of Christian professions—who take every tenderness their wives bring them, and every expression of affection, and every service, and every yearning sympathy, and trample them under feet without tasting them, and without a look of gratitude in their eyes. Hard, cold, thin-blooded, white-livered, contemptible curmudgeons—they think their wives weak and foolish, and themselves wise and dignified! I beg my readers to assist me in despising them. I do not feel adequate to the task of doing them justice.

There is another exhibition of perverseness which we sometimes see in families. There will be, perhaps, from two to half a dozen sisters in a family, amiable all of them. Now, think of the reasons which should bind them together in the tenderest sympathy. They were born of the same mother, they were nursed at the same heart, they were cradled under the same roof by the same hand, they have knelt at the side of the same father, their interests, trials, associates, standing—every thing concerning their family and social life—are the same. The honor of one intimately concerns the honor of the other, yet I have known such families of sisters fly apart the moment they became in any way independent of each other, as if they were natural enemies. I have seen them take the part of a friend against any member of the family band, and become disgusted with one another's society. Where matters have not gone to this length, I have seen sisters who would never caress each other, or, by any but the most formal and dignified methods, express their affection for each other. I have seen them live together for months and years as inexpressive of affection for each other as cattle in a stall,—more so: for I have seen a cow affectionately lick her neighbor's ear by the half-hour, while among these girls I have failed to see a kiss, or hear a tender word, or witness any exhibition of sisterly affection whatever.

One of the most common forms of perverseness, though one of the most subtle and least known, is that shown by people who study to shut everybody out from a knowledge of their nature and their life. They make it their grand end and aim to appear to be exactly what they are not, to appear to believe exactly what they do not believe, and to appear to feel what they do not feel at all. This is not because they are ashamed of themselves, or because they really have any thing to conceal. They have simply taken on this form of perverseness. They will not, if they can help it, allow any man to get inside of their natures and characters. If they write you a letter, they will mislead you. They will say to you irreverent and shocking things, to prove to you that they are bold, and unfeeling, and unthoughtful, when they tremble at what they have written, and really show by their language that they are afraid, and full of feeling, and very thoughtful. If they have a sentiment of love for anybody, they take it as a dog would a bone, and go and dig a hole in the ground and bury it, only resorting to it in the dark, for private craunching. Very likely they will try to make you believe that they live a most dainty and delicate life —that the animals of the field, and the fowls of the air love them, and come at their call—that clouds arrange themselves in heaven for their benefit, and are sufficiently paid for the effort by their admiration—that flowers excite them to frenzy—a very fine frenzy, indeed—and that all sounds shape themselves to music in their souls. They would have you think that they live a kind of charmed life—that the sun woos them, and the moon pines for them, and the sea sobs because they will not come, and the daisies wait lovingly for their feet, yet, if you knew the truth, you would see that they sit discontentedly among the homeliest surroundings of domestic life, with their sleeves rolled up—confound them!

This variety of perverseness seems very inexplicable. I have seen much of it, but do not know what to make of it. There is doubtless something morbid in it. It is often carried to such extremes, and managed so artfully, that multitudes are deceived by it. I know of some very beautiful natures that pass in the world for rough and coarse. I know men who have the reputation of being hard and harsh, yet who are, inside, and in their own consciousness, as gentle and sensitive as women—who put on a stern air and a repellent manner, when they are really yearning for sympathy. I have seen this air and manner broken through and battered down by a friendly man, who found what he suspected behind it—a generous, warm, noble heart. This perverseness seems to be akin to that of the miser who knows he is rich, takes his highest delight in being rich, and yet dresses meanly, and fares like a beggar rather than be thought rich. Women hide themselves more than men. They are generally more sensitive, and their life and circumscribed habits have a tendency to the formation of morbid moods, and this among the number.

Of the perverseness of partisanship in politics much is written, and my pen need not dip into it; but there is a perverseness exhibited by Christian churches in their quarrels that should be exposed and discussed, because some people have an impression that it may possibly be piety. "For *dum squizzle*, read *permanence*," said an editor, correcting a typographical error that had found its way into his journal. It seems as strange that perverseness should be mistaken for piety, as that "permanence" should be mistaken for "dum squizzle," but I believe it often is. Let some little cause of disturbance arise, and become active in a church, and it is astonishing how both parties go to work and pray over it. The pastor, perhaps, has said something on the subject of slavery, or he does not preach doctrine enough, or he preaches the wrong sort of doctrine, or he does not visit his people enough, or there is "a row" about the singing, or about a change in the hymn-books, or about repairing the church, or buying an organ, or something or other, and straightway sides are taken, and the wills of both parties get roused. It is sometimes laughable—it would always be, only that it is too sad—to see how quickly both parties grow pious, as they grow perverse. It would seem, as the strife waxes hot, that the glory of God was never so much in their hearts as now. They pray with fervor, they are constant in their public religious duties, they pass through the most scrupulous self-examinations, and then fight on to the bitter end; believing, I suppose, that they are really doing God service, when they are only gratifying their own perverse wills.

Churches have been ruined, or divided, or crippled in their power, by a cause of quarrel too insignificant to engage the minds of sensible worldly men for an hour. I have heard it said that church quarrels are the most violent of all quarrels, because religious feelings are the strongest feelings of our nature. I confess that I do not see the force of this statement, for it does not appear to me that religious feelings have much to do with these quarrels. I can much more easily see why all personal differences should be adjusted peaceably in a church, for there it is supposed that the individual will is subordinated to the cause of religion and the general good. The real basis of the bitterness of church quarrels is women. There are no others, except neighborhood quarrels, in which women mingle, and a neighborhood quarrel will at once be recognized as more like a church quarrel than any other. Women have strong feelings, are attracted or repulsed through their sensibilities, conceive keen likes and dislikes, do not stop to reason, and are, of course, the readiest and the most devoted partisans. If the mouths of the women could only be smothered in a church quarrel, it would be settled much easier. Of all the perverse creatures in this world, a woman who has thoroughly committed herself to any man, or any cause, is the least tractable and reasonable. I hope this statement will not offend my sweet friends, because it is so true that I cannot conscientiously retract it.

What the books call pride of opinion, is, nine cases in ten, simple perverseness. I know a most venerable public teacher of physiology, whose early theory of the production of animal heat—very ridiculous in itself—is still yearly announced from his desk, notwithstanding the fact that the whole world has received another, whose soundness is demonstrated beyond all question. As he, year after year, declares his belief that animal heat is produced by corpuscular friction in the circulating blood, there is a twinkle of the eyes among his amused auditors which says very plainly—"the old gentleman does not believe this, himself." The youngest student before him knows better than to give his theory a moment's consideration. Well, the old Doctor is not alone. The world is full of this kind of thing. Men adhere to old opinions and old policies long after they have learned that they are shallow or untenable, not from a genuine pride of opinion, (I doubt very much whether there really is any thing that should be called pride of opinion,) but from genuine perverseness of disposition. Men will give, in some heated moment, an opinion touching some one's character or powers, and, though that opinion be proved to be wrong a thousand times, they will never acknowledge that they have made a mistake. This is simple perverseness, of the meanest variety. There are some kinds of perverseness which impress one not altogether unpleasantly, but this affects a man with equal anger and disgust.

Perverseness is a sign of weakness—nay, an element of weakness—in man or woman. It is no legitimate part of a true character. The generous, outspoken man, who is not afraid to show himself, and what there is in him, who cares more about the right way than his way, who throws away an opinion as he would throw away an old hat, the moment he finds it is worthless, and who good-naturedly allows the frictions of society to straighten out all the kinks there are in him, is the strong man always, and always the one whom men love. Perverseness is really moral strabismus, and I am shocked to think what a multitude of squint-eyed souls there will be, when we come to look into one another's faces in the "undress of immortality."

LESSON X.

UNDEVELOPED RESOURCES.

"The world is God's seed-bed. He has planted deep and multitudinously, and many things there are which have not yet come up."—BEECHER.

ONE of the richest and best of the smaller class of American cities is New Bedford; and the secret of its wealth and beauty is *oil.* It is but a few years since the immense fleet of vessels that made that thrifty port their home went out with certainty of success in their dangerous enterprises, and came back loaded down with spoil. All that beautiful wealth was won from the deep, and for years as many ships came and went as there were dwellings to give them speed and welcome. But the glory and the gain of the whale-fishery are past. The noble prey, too persistently and mercilessly pursued, has retired northward, and hidden among the icebergs. Now, when a ship's crew win a cargo, they win it from the clutches of eternal frost.

It seems certain that the fishery will dwindle, year after year, until, at last, only a few adventurers will linger near the pole, to watch for the rare game that once furnished light for the civilized world. All this is very unpleasant for New Bedford; but are we to have no more oil? Is nature failing? Will the time come when people must sit in darkness?

A few months ago a man in Pennsylvania took it into his head to probe the ground for the source of a certain oil that made its appearance upon the surface. Down, down into the bowels of the earth he thrust his steam-driven harpoon, until he touched the living fountain of oil, which, gushing up, half drowned him. Now, all the region round about him swarms with industry. Thousands of men are hurrying to and fro; the puff of the engine is heard everywhere; tens of thousands of barrels of oil are rolled out and turned into the channels of commerce; eager-eyed speculators throng all the converging avenues of travel, and a waiting world of consumers take the oil as fast as it is produced. Men in Virginia, New York, and Ohio are awaking to the consciousness that, while they have been paying for oil from the far Pacific, they have been living within three hundred feet of deposits greater than all the cargoes that ever floated in New Bedford harbor. For hundreds, and, probably, for thousands of years, men have walked over these deposits with no suspicion of their existence. Geologists have looked wise, as is their habit, but have given no hint of them.

The simple truth appears to be that when, in the history of the world, it became necessary for these firmly-fastened store-houses of oil to be uncovered, they were uncovered. Nature had held them for untold thousands of years for just this emergency. When the whales ceased spouting, the earth took up the business; and "here she blows" and "there she blows" are heard in Tideoute and Titusville, while New Bedford sits sadly by the sea, and thinks of long absent crews to whom the cry has become strange.

I cannot but look upon this discovery of oil in the earth as one of the most remarkable and instructive revelations of the age. It has shown to me that, whenever human necessity demands any thing of the world of matter, the demand will be honored. Whenever animal life, or the muscle of man or brute, has shown itself unequal to the wants of an age, Nature has always responded to the cry for help. Inventors are only men who act as pioneers, and who go forward to see what the human race will want next, and to make the necessary provisions. An inventor has profound faith in the exhaustless resources of nature. He knows that if he bores far enough, and bores in the right direction, he will find that which the world needs. He is often no more than the discoverer of a secret which nature has kept for the satisfaction of the wants of an age. A lake yoked to a coal-bed would generally be voted a slow team, but the inventor of the steam engine saw how it could be made a very fast and a very powerful one; and we who live now are able to see that the discovery was made at the right time, and that, for the emergencies of this latter day, it has really quadrupled the power of civilized man.

Think how nature has risen grandly up to meet every occasion for new resources. The revolution wrought by steam in the business of the world created great wants, every one of which was filled as soon as felt. Quicker modes of communicating thought were needed to give us all the advantages of the increased facility of carriage, and Mr. Morse was permitted to uncover the telegraph. More money was wanted for the increased business of the world, and the gold fields of California and Australia were unveiled. It has always been so. In the march of the human race along the track of history, nature has pulled aside the veil in which she hides her treasures, to display that which she has kept in store for every epoch. In all the future I have no doubt that whenever oil shall be wanted, oil will be had for the boring. The world is fitted up with supplies for all the probable and possible wants of the human race. We are treading every day upon the lids of great secrets that await the wants of the larger style and finer type of life that lie before us. Discovery has but just begun, and will, I doubt not, be as rife in future ages as in this. There is no end of it: yet the world is a thing to be weighed and measured. It is so many miles around it, and so many miles through it. Never mind; it has more in it than humanity can exhaust.

When we talk of the material world, especially in its relation to the constantly developing wants of man, we talk simply of the kitchen and larder of humanity. We have not ascended into the drawing-room, or conservatory. The moment we step out of the consideration of manifested nature, we come into a world which may neither be weighed nor measured—the world of thought. I suppose that no author has ever entered a large library and stood in its alcoves and studied its titles long without asking himself the question: "what is there left for me to do?" It seems as if men had been reaching in all directions for the discovery of thought since time began, and as if there were absolutely nothing new to be said upon any subject. Yet every age has always demanded its peculiar food, and every age has managed to get it. Certain great and peculiarly fruitful subjects, blowing in the sea of thought, have attracted whole fleets of authors for many years, and they are doubtless chased away no more to return; but, here and there, while time shall last, strong men will bore down to deposits of thought unsuspected by any of the preceding generations of men, and there will gush up streams to light the nations of the world. For the world of thought is, by its nature, exhaustless. The world of thought is the world in which God lives, and it is infinite like himself. We reach our hands out into the dark in any direction, and find a thought. It was God's before it was ours; and on beyond that thought, lies another, and still another, *ad infinitum.* If our arms were long enough, we should be able to grasp them as well as the first. All that it wants is the long arm to give us the command of deposits that would astonish the world. Authors have become eminent according to their power to reach further than others out into the infinite atmosphere of thought which envelops them.

Authors, like inventors, are rarely more than discoverers. If God, who is omniscient, sees all truth, and apprehends the relations of every truth to every other truth, all an author can do is, of course, to find out what God's thoughts are. And every age is certain to find out the thought that is essential to it. When the world had exhausted Aristotle, and the wide school of philosophers who embraced him in their systems, Bacon, self-instituted, stepped before the world as its teacher. He came when he was wanted, and his age gave him audience, and took the better path which he pointed out to it. It was in the golden age of the drama—the age in which the drama was what it never was before, and will never be again—a great agent of civilization—that Shakspeare appeared. We call his plays creations, but surely they were not his. He no more than discovered them. The reason why they stir us so much is that God created them. His age wanted them, and he had the insight into the world of thought which enabled him to enter in and lead them out. The reason why we have not had any great dramatist since, is, that succeeding ages have not needed one. The great men of later ages have not recognized the drama as a want of their particular time. I am aware that there is nothing in this to feed human pride, but I do not recognize food for human pride as a want of any age.

We are in the habit of talking of the old authors; and we read them as if we supposed them wiser than ourselves. We try to feed on the thought which they discovered, but it is in the main very innutritious fodder, and the world is learning the fact. We read and reverence old books less, and read and regard newspapers a great deal more. The thought which our own age produces is that which we are learning to prize most. We buy beautiful editions of Scott, but we read Dickens and Thackeray and Mrs. Stowe, in weekly and monthly numbers. Milton, in half-calf, stands upon the shelves of our library undisturbed, while we cut the leaves of "Festus;" and Keats and Byron and Shelley are all pushed aside that we may converse with Longfellow and Mrs. Browning. It is not, perhaps, that the later are the greater, but, being informed with the spirit of the age in which we have our life, moving among the facts which concern us, and conscious of our want, they apprehend the true relations of their age to the world of thought around them. They see where the sources of oil are exhausted, and bore for new deposits. It is a comfort to know that they can never bore in vain.

We may be sure that literature will always be as fresh as it has been. It is possible that we may never have greater men than Shakspeare and Milton, and Dante and Goethe; but there is nothing to hinder our having men just as great. Those who are to come will only bore in different directions, and find new deposits. Shakspeare and Milton were great writers, but the fields they occupied were their own. They do not resemble each other in any particular. Dante nd Goethe were great writers, but there are no points of resemblance between them. When Scott was issuing his wonderful series of novels, it seemed to his cotemporaries, I suppose, that there was no field left for a successor; yet Dickens, in the next generation, won as many readers and as much admiration as he, in a field whose existence Scott never suspected. Very different is the world of thought from the world of matter, in the fact that its deposits are found in no particular spot. The mind can go out in quest of thought in no direction without reward; and every man receives from his age motive and culture which peculiarly prepare him for the work of supplying its needs. There are some who seem to think that the golden age of literature is past—that nothing modern is worthy of notice, and that it is one of the vices of the age that we discard so much the teachings of the literary fathers. But the world of thought is exhaustless, and we have only to produce a finer civilization than the world has ever seen, to secure, as its consummate flower, a literature of corresponding excellence.

What has been said of the world of matter and the world of thought, may be said, and is implied, of the world of men. We are accustomed to say that great emergencies make great men. But this is not true. Great men are always found to meet great emergencies: but God makes them, and leads them through a course of discipline which prepares them for their work. It is one of the remarkable facts of history, so patent that all have seen and acknowledged it, that to meet every great epoch a man has been prepared. I mean it in no irreverent or theological sense when I say that there has been a series of Christs, whose appearance has denoted the departure of old dispensations and the inauguration of new. Men have arisen who have torn down temples, and demolished idols, and swept away systems, and knocked off fetters, and introduced their age into a freer, better, and larger life; and it will always be so while time shall last. Men will arise equal to the wants of their age wherever men are civilized. The causes which produce emergencies are the agents which educate men to meet them; and nature is prodigal of her material among men, as among the things made for his service.

When, in the history of Christianity, it became necessary to re-assert and emphasize the truth that "the just shall live by faith," Luther was raised up; and nothing is more apparent to the student than that the age which produced him demanded him—that he fitted into his age, supplied its wants, and cut a new channel, through which the richest life of the world has flowed for centuries. He found his country tied up to formalism, scholasticism, and tradition; and by strokes as remarkable for boldness as strength he set it free. He stands at the head of a great historical epoch, which was prepared to receive and crown him. In another field, we have, even in this day, a reformer whom his age has called for, and who will surely do in the world of art what Luther did in religion. No one can read Ruskin, and mark his enthusiasm, his splendid power, his earnestness, his love of truth, his reverence for nature, and above all, his love of God, without feeling that he has a great mission to fulfil in the world. I bow myself in homage before this man, and acknowledge his credentials. He speaks with authority, and not as the common run of scribes, at all. Fearlessly he tears the mask away from conventionalism and pretension, sparing neither age nor nation, and scattering critics right and left

> "Like chaff from the threshing-floor."

It seems to me that the sight of this single, unsupported man, plunging boldly into a fight with a whole world full of liars and lies, thrusting right and left, anxious only for the triumph of truth, and everywhere devoutly recognizing God and his glory, and Christ and his honor, as the ultimate end of true art, is one of the most striking and beautiful the world has ever seen. Was there not need of him? Had not art become superstitious and infidel and missionless? Had it not faded to little more than the repetition of old inanities, traditional mannerisms, stereotyped lies? Ruskin came to tell his age that art was doing nothing toward making the world better—that, instead of lifting the heart toward God, and enlarging the field of human sympathy, it was only ministering to the vanity of men—that nature was dishonored that men might win the applause of vulgar crowds by falsehood and trickery. Nobly has he done and nobly is he still doing his work; and the world is reading him. It matters not that critics carp, and scold, and whine—the world is reading, and will regard him. The eternal truth of God and nature is on his side; and we are to see, as I firmly believe, resulting from his noble labors, a beautiful resurrection of art from the grave in which its friends have laid it. It shall come forth, though now bound hand and foot, and be restored to the sisterhood whose happiness it is to serve and sit at the feet of Jesus Christ.

But time and space would fail to give illustrations of the truth that God has always a man ready for an emergency. It is not necessary to speak of Washington. It would not be wise, perhaps, to speak of the first Napoleon, because men differ so widely in their estimate of his work. But of the last Napoleon, it may be said that he furnishes one of the most notable instances the world has ever seen of a man prepared for his age. I suppose that no one believes that there is another man in existence who could have done for France, and would have done for Europe, under the circumstances, what Louis Napoleon has done. Never did the central figure of an elaborate piece of mosaic fit more nicely into its place, than did Louis Napoleon into the complicated affairs of his age. They were made for him, and he for them.

Shall the world of matter never fail—shall the world of thought be exhaustless—shall men be found for all the emergencies of their race, and, yet, shall divine truth be contained in a nut-shell? Must the human soul lack food—fresh food—because a generation long gone has decided that only certain food is fit for the human soul? I believe that the Bible is a revelation of divine truth to men, and, believing this, I believe that its most precious deposits have hardly been touched. I believe that in it, there is special food prepared for all the wide variety of human souls, and that, as generation after generation passes away, new deposits will be struck, so rich in illuminating power that their discoverers will wonder they had never been seen before. I know that just before me, or somewhere before me, there is a generation of men who will think less of being saved, and more of being worth saving, less of dogma, and more of duty, less of law, and more of love; whose worship will be less formal, and more truthful and spiritual, and whose God will be a more tender and considerate father, and less a lawgiver and a judge. For such a generation, there exists a deposit of divine truth almost unknown by Christendom. Only here and there have men gathered it, floating upon the surface. The great deposit waits the touch of another age.

LESSON XI.

GREATNESS IN LITTLENESS.

"This earth will all its dust and tears
Is no less his than yonder spheres;
And rain-drops weak and grains of sand
Are stamped by his immediate hand."
STERLING.

"There is a power
Unseen, that rules the illimitable world;
That guides its motions, from the brightest star
To the least dust of this sin-tainted world."
THOMSON.

INFINITY lies below us as well as above us. There is as much essential greatness in littleness as in largeness. Mont Blanc—massive, ice-crowned, imperial—is a great work of nature; yet it is only an aggregation of materials with which we are thoroughly familiar. It is only a larger mountain than that which lies within sight of my window. A dozen Monadnocks or Ascutneys or Holyokes, more or less, make a Mont Blanc, with glaciers and avalanches and brooding eternity of frost. Such greatness, though it impresses me much, is not beyond my comprehension. It can be reckoned by cubic miles. So with the sea: it is only an expanse of water larger than the river that winds through the meadows. It is great, but it is only an aggregate of numerable quantities that my eyes can measure, and my mind comprehend. These are great objects, and they are great particularly because they are large. They are above me, and they lead me upward toward creative infinity.

If I turn my eyes in the other direction, however, I lose myself in infinity quite as readily. If I pick up a pebble at the foot of Mont Blanc, and undertake the examination of its structure,—the elements which compose it, the relations of those elements to each other, the mode of their combination—I am lost as readily as I should be in following the footsteps of the stars. If I undertake to look through a drop of water, I may be arrested at first, indeed, by the sports and struggles of animalcular life; but at length I find myself gazing beyond it into infinitude—using it as a lens through which the Godhead becomes visible to me. I can dissect from one another the muscles and arteries and veins and nerves and vital viscera of the human body, but the little insect that taps a vein upon my hand does it with an instrument and by the operation of machinery which are beyond my scrutiny. They belong to a life and are the servants of instincts which I do not understand at all.

These thoughts come to me, borne by certain memories. I know a venerable gentleman of Buffalo—Dr. Scott—who did, and who still does, very great things in a very small way. At the age of seventy he became conscious of decaying power of vision. Being professionally a physician and naturally a philosopher, he conceived the idea that the eye might be improved by what he denominated a series of "ocular gymnastics." He therefore undertook to exercise his eyes upon the formation of minute letters—working upon them until the organs began to be weary, and then, like a prudent man, resting for hours. By progressing slowly and carefully, he became, at last, able to do wonders in the way of fine writing, and also became able to read the newspapers without glasses. (Here's a hint for some clever Yankee—as good as a fortune.) Now, reader, prepare for a large story; but be assured that it is true, and that my hands have handled and my eyes seen the things of which I tell you. At the age of seventy-one, Dr. Scott wrote upon an enamelled card with a stile, on space exactly equal to that of one side of a three-cent piece,—The Lord's Prayer, the Apostles' Creed, the Parable of the Ten Virgins, the Parable of the Rich Man and Lazarus, the Beatitudes, the fifteenth Psalm, the one hundred and twentieth Psalm, the one hundred and thirty-third Psalm, the one hundred and thirty-first Psalm, and the figures "1860." Every word, every letter, and every point, of all these passages was written exquisitely on this minute space; and that old man not only saw every mark he made, but had the delicacy of muscular action and steadiness of nerve to form the letters so beautifully that they abide the test of the highest magnifying power. They were, of course, written by microscopic aid.

Now who believes that it does not require more genius and skill to execute this minute work than it does to bore a Hoosac tunnel, or build a Victoria bridge, or put a dam across the Connecticut, or construct an Erie canal? I do not speak of the relative importance of the great works and the small, but of the relative amount and quality of the power that is brought to bear upon them. In a very important sense the greatest thing a man can do is the most difficult thing he can do. The most difficult thing a man can do may not be the most useful, or in any sense the most important; but it will measure and show the limits of his power. Work grows difficult as it goes below a man, quite as rapidly as it does when it rises above him. It costs as much skill to make a dainty bit of jewelry as it does to carve a colossal statue. It actually costs more power to make the chain of gold that holds the former, than it does to forge the clumsy links by which the latter is dragged to its location. Thus, whether man goes down or up, he soon gets beyond the sphere of his power. The further he can carry himself in either direction the more does he demonstrate his superiority over the majority of men. The more difficult the task which he performs the further does he reach toward infinity.

In the town of Waltham there is a manufactory of watches which I have examined with great interest. It is here undertaken to organize the skill which has been achieved by thousands of patient hands, and submit it to machinery; and it is done. Every thing is so systematized, and the operations are carried on with such exactness, that, among a hundred watches, corresponding parts may be interchanged without embarrassment to the machinery. The different parts are passed from hand to hand, and from machine to machine, each hand and each machine simply doing its duty, and when from different and distant rooms these parts are assembled, and cunning fingers put them together, every wheel knows its place, and every pivot and every screw its home, though it be picked without discrimination from a dish containing ten thousand. Yet among these parts there are screws of which it takes one hundred and fifty thousand to make a pound, and shafts and bearings which are so delicately turned that five thousand shavings will only extend a lineal inch along the steel. This is the way American watches are made, and this is the way in which the highest practicable perfection is reached in the manufacture of these pocket monitors.

Here we have small work, organized, and great elaboration of related details. When Dr. Scott wrote his passages on the card, his work was very simple. He did only one thing—he made letters. When he had made letter after letter until the little space was filled, his work was done. It was not a part of some complicated and inter-dependent whole, related to a thousand other parts in other hands. I suppose it may be as delicate work to drill a jewel with a hair of steel, armed with paste of diamond-dust, as to write "Our Father" under a microscope; but when the jewel has to be drilled with relation to the reception of a revolving metallic pivot, the process becomes very much nicer. So here are a hundred processes going on at the same time, in different parts of a building, all related to each other, each delicate almost beyond description, and effected with such precision that a mistake is so much an exception that it is a surprise. I have seen the huge steam engines at Scranton which furnish power for the blast of the furnaces there, and their magnitude and power and most impressive majesty of movement have made me tremble; yet as works of man they are no greater than a Waltham watch.

It seems to me that man occupies a position just half way between infinite greatness and infinite littleness, and that he can neither ascend nor descend to any considerable degree without bringing up against a wall which shows where man ends and God begins. It seems, too, that that kind of human power which can reach down deepest into the infinite littleness, is more remarkable than that which rises highest toward the infinite greatness. It is a more difficult and a more remarkable thing to write the Lord's Prayer on a single line less than an inch long, than it would be to paint it on the face of the Palisades, upon a line a mile long, in letters the length of the painter's ladder. I have heard of a watch so small that it was set in a ring, and worn upon the finger; and such a watch seems very much more marvellous to me than the engines of the Great Eastern.

We are in the habit of regarding God as the author of all the great movements of the universe, but as having nothing to do directly with the minor movements. Mr. Emerson becomes equally flippant and irreverent when he speaks of a "pistareen Providence." We kindly take the Creator and upholder of all things under our patronage, and say, "it is very well for him to swing a star into space, and set bounds to the sea, and order the goings of great systems, and even to minister to the lives of great men, but when it comes to meddling with the little affairs of the daily life of a thousand millions of men, women, and children—pshaw! He's above all that."

Not so fast, Mr. Emerson! The real reason why you and all those who are like you do not believe in God's intimate cognizance and administration of human affairs is, that you cannot comprehend them. You have not faith enough in God to believe that he is able to maintain this knowledge of human affairs, this interest in them, and the power and the disposition to mould them to divine issues. You are willing to admit that God can do a few great things, but you are not willing to admit that he can do a great many little things. It is well enough, according to your notion, for God to make a mastodon, or a megatherium, but quite undignified for him to undertake a mosquito or a horse-fly. It would not compromise His reputation with you were you to catch Him lighting a sun, or watching with something of interest the rise and fall of a great nation, but actually to listen to the prayer of a little child, and to answer that prayer with distinctness of purpose and definite exercise of power, would not, in your opinion, be dignified and respectable business for a being whom you are proud to have the honor of worshipping!

I do not know how these people who do not believe in the intimate special providence of God can believe in God at all. I can conceive how God could rear Mont Blanc, but I cannot conceive how He could make a honey bee, and endow that honey bee with an instinct—transmitted since the creation from bee to bee, and swarm to swarm—which binds it in membership to a commonwealth, and enables it to build its waxen cells with mathematical exactness, and gather honey from all the flowers of the field. It is when we go into the infinity below us that the infinite power and skill become the most evident. When the microscope shows us life in myriad forms, each of which exhibits design; when we contemplate vegetable life in its wonderful details; when chemistry reveals to us something of the marvellous processes by which vitality is fed, we get a more impressive sense of the power and skill of the Creator than we do when we turn the telescope toward the heavens. Yet Mr. Emerson would have us believe that the Being who saw fit to make all these little things, to arrange and throw into relation all these masses of detail, to paint the plumage of a bird, and the back of a fly, as richly as he paints the drapery of the descending sun, does not condescend to take practical interest in the affairs of men and women! My God, what blindness! Bird, bee, blossom—be my teacher. I do not like Mr. Emerson's lesson.

The logical sequence of disbelief in what Mr. Emerson calls a "pistareen Providence" is a belief in pantheism or polytheism. There is certainly nothing ridiculous in the faith that the Being who contrived and arranged, and adjusted the infinite littlenesses of creation, and ordained their laws, and who continues their existence, maintains an intimate interest in the only intelligent creatures he has placed in this world. The little bird that sings to me, the bee that bears me honey, the blossom that brings me perfume, all testify to me that He who created them will not neglect nor forget His own child. If I look up into the firmament, and send my imagination into its deep abysses, and think that further than even dreams can go, those abysses are strewn with stars; if I think of comets coming and going with the rush of lightning, and yet occupying whole centuries in their journey; or if I only sit down by the sea, and think of the waves that kiss other shores thousands of miles away, I am oppressed by a sense of my own littleness. I ask the question whether the God who has such large things in His care, can think of me—a speck on an infinite aggregate of surface—a mote uneasily shifting in the boundless space. I get no hope in this direction; but I look down, and find that the shoulders of all inferior creation are under me, lifting me into the very presence of God. I find that God has been at work below me, in a mass of minute and munificent detail, by the side of which my life is great and simple, and satisfyingly significant.

So, if I may not believe in a "pistareen Providence," I must make a God of the universe itself, or pass into the hands of many Gods the world's creation and governance. If the God that made the bee, and the ant, and the daisy, made me, then He is not above taking care of me, and of maintaining an interest in the smallest affairs of my life. The faith that lives in reason is never stronger than when it stands on flowers. There is not a fly that floats, nor a fish that swims, nor an animalcule that navigates its little drop of sea-spray, but bears a burden of hope to despairing humanity. "If God so clothe the grass which to-day is, and to-morrow is cast into the oven," then what, Mr. Emerson?

This subject is a very large one, and I can present only one more phase of it. A great multitude—the larger part, in fact—of the human race are engaged in doing small work. It may be a comfort for them to know that the Almighty Maker of all things has done a great deal of the same kind of work, and has not found it unworthy or unprofitable employment. Let them remember that it is just as hard to do a small thing well as a large thing, and that the difficulty of a deed is the gauge of the power required for its doing. Let them remember that when they go down, they are going just as directly toward infinity as when they go up, and that every man who works Godward, works in honor.

It was a very forcible reflection to which a visitor at Niagara Falls gave utterance, when he said that, considering the relative power of their authors, he did not regard the cataract as so remarkable a piece of work as the Suspension Bridge; and it may be said with truth that there is no work within the power of man so small that God has not been below it in a work smaller and possibly humbler still,—certainly humbler when we consider the infinite majesty and the ineffable dignity of His character. My maid is too proud to go into the street for a pail of milk; my God smiles upon me in flowers from the very gutter. My neighbor thinks it beneath him to till the soil, working with his hands, but the Being who made him, breathes upon that soil, and works in it, that it may bear food to keep human dignity from starving. There are men who set themselves above driving a horse, no part of which the King of the universe was above making. Ah! human pride! Alas! human dignity! I do not know what to make of you.

LESSON XII.

RURAL LIFE.

"Going into a village at night, with the lights gleaming on each side of the street, in some houses they will be in the basement and nowhere else."

BEECHER.

"The little God o' the world jogs on the same old way,
And is as singular as on the world's first day.
A pity 'tis thou shouldst have given
The fool, to make him worse, a gleam of light from heaven;
He calls it reason, using it
To be more beast than ever beast was yet.
He seems to me, (your grace the words will pardon,)
Like a long-legged grasshopper, in the garden,
Forever on the wing, and hops and sings
The same old song, as in the grass he springs."

GOETHE'S FAUST.

IT is a common remark that a railroad car is an excellent place in which to study human nature; but the particular phase of human nature which is usually presented there is not, I think, sufficiently attractive to engage a man who desires to maintain a good opinion of his race. I would as soon think of studying human nature in a pig-pen as in a railroad car. I do not like to study even my own nature there, for I find that the more I ride, the more selfish I become, and the more desirable it seems to me that I should occupy the space usually assigned to four men, viz.: two seats for my feet, and two for such other portions of my person as are not required for spanning the space between the sofas. It must be a matter of regret to most persons, I am sure, that they are not large enough to cover twice as many seats as they do, and thus drive those who travel with them into more close and inconvenient quarters. Whenever I witness an instance of genuine, self-sacrificing politeness in a railroad car, I become aware that there is at least one man on the train who has travelled very little. No; when I travel I turn my observation upon things outside—upon the farms and streams, and mountains and forests, and towns and villages through which the train bears me. I am particularly interested in the faces of those who gather at the smaller stations to gaze at the passengers, get the papers, and feel the rush, for a single moment, of the world's great life. I love to listen to the smart remarks of some rustic wit in shirt-sleeves, who, if the train should happen to be behind time, intimates to the brakeman that the old horse didn't have his allowance of oats that morning, or commiserates the loneliness of the conductor of a train not crowded with passengers,—all of which is intended for the ears of a village girl who stands in the door of the "Ladies' Room," with the tip of a parasol in her teeth, and a hat on her head that was jaunty last year.

Riding into the country recently, I saw at one of these little stations a pair of young men, leaning against the station-house. They had evidently been waiting for the approach of the train, but they did not stir from their positions. They were young men whose life had been spent in severe and unremitting toil. Their hands were large, and coarse, and brown; their faces and necks were bronzed; their clothing was of the commonest material and pattern, and was old and patched besides; and they had a hard look generally. There was the usual bustle about them, but they did not seem to mind it. At last, they started, and these are the words that one of them spoke: "Come, Bob, let's go over and see if we can't tuck away some of that grub." So both turned their backs upon the train, and upon me; and as they went over to see if they couldn't "tuck away some of that grub," I got a view of their heavy shoulders, and their shambling, awkward gait. A pair of old draft horses, going out in the morning to take their places in front of their truck, would not move more stiffly than those fellows moved.

Now these young men taught me nothing, for I had seen many such before; but through them I took a fresh and a very impressive glimpse into a style of life that abounds among the rural population of America, and shows but feeble signs of improvement. These men, who, when they eat, only "tuck away grub," of course "go to roost" when they sleep. They call the sun "Old Yaller," naming him in honor of a favorite ox. When they undress themselves "they peel off," as if they were onions or potatoes; and when they put themselves into their Sunday clothing, they "surprise their backs with a clean shirt." When they marry, they "hitch on," as if matrimony were a sled, and a wife were a saw-log. Every thing in their life is brought down to the animal basis, and why should it not be? They labor as severely as any animal they own; they are proud of their animal strength and endurance; they eat, and work, and sleep, like animals, and they do nothing like men. Their frames are shaped by labor; and they are only the best animals, and the ruling animals, on their farms. As between the wives and children who live in their houses, and the horses and cattle that live in their barns, the latter have the easier time of it.

Having brought every thing down to the animal basis in their homes and in their lives, their intercourse with other men will naturally betray the ideas upon which they live. They are usually very blunt men, who "never go round" to say any thing, but who blurt out what they have to say in a manner entirely regardless of the feelings of others. They enter each other's houses with their hats on, and "help themselves" when they sit at each other's tables, and affect great contempt for the courtesies and forms of polite life. They are exceedingly afraid of being looked upon as "stuck up;" and if they can get the reputation of being able to mow more grass, or pitch more hay, or chop and pile more wood, or cradle more grain, than any of their neighbors, their ambition is satisfied. There is no dignity of life in their homes. They cook and eat and live in the same room, and sometimes sleep there, if there should be room enough for a bed. There is no family life that is not associated with work, and no thought of any life that is not connected with bodily labor; and if they sit down five minutes, either at home or at church, they go to sleep. Their highest intellectual exercise is that which is called out by the process of swapping horses, and the selling of their weekly product of eggs and butter at the highest market price. They invariably call their wives—"the old woman," or "she;" and if they should stumble into saying, "my dear," in the presence of a neighbor, they would blush at being self-convicted of unjustifiable politeness and unpardonable weakness.

These men have learned to read, but they rarely read any thing, except the weekly newspaper, taken exclusively for the probate notices. The only books in their houses are the Bible and two or three volumes forced upon them at unguarded moments by book-agents, who made the most of internal wood-cuts, and external Dutch metal to place them in possession of the "History of the World," or the "Lives of the Presidents," or some other production equally extensive and comprehensive. There is no exhibition of taste about their dwellings. Every thing is brought down to the hard standard of use. If their wives should desire a border for flowers, they regard them as very silly, and look upon their attempts to "fix up things" as a great waste of labor. They never go out with their wives to mingle in the social life of their neighborhood; and if the wives of their neighbors come to spend an afternoon, they harness their horses, and drive off to attend to some distant business that will detain them until the women get away. It is useless to say to me that this is an extreme picture, for I know what I am writing about, and know that I am painting from the life. I know that there are hundreds of thousands of American farmers whose life and whose ideas of life are cast upon these models. Some of these are as coarse and hard as I paint them, and others are only a little better.

Such a farmer's boy is brought up to the idea that work is the grand thing in life. Work, indeed, is supposed by him to be pretty much all of life. It is supposed to spoil farmers to get any thing but work into their heads; and scientific agriculturists will bear witness that they have been obliged to fight the popular prejudices against "book farming" at every step of their progress. They will also testify that the improvements made in farming and in the implements of agriculture have not been made by farmers themselves, but by outsiders—mechanics, and men of science—who have marvelled at the brainless stupidity which toiled on in its old track of unreasoning routine, and looked with suspicion and discouragement upon innovations. The reason why the farmer has not been foremost in improving the instruments and methods of his own business, is, that his mind has been unfitted for improvement by the excessive labors of his body. A man whose whole vital energy is directed to the support of muscle has, of course, none to direct to the support of thought. A man whose strength is habitually exhausted by bodily labor becomes, at length, incapable of mental exertion; and I cannot help feeling that half of the farmers of the country establish insuperable obstacles to their own improvement by their excessive toil. They are nothing more than the living machines of a calling which so far exhausts their vitality that they have neither the disposition nor the power to improve either their calling or themselves.

To a student or a literary man, it is easy to explain

the necessity of the proper division of the nervous energies between the mind and the body. Any student or literary man who has a daily mental task to do, will do it before he exercises his body to any great extent. If I wished to unfit my mind for a day of literary labor, I would use the hoe in my garden for an early hour in the morning. If I wished utterly to unfit a pupil for his daily task of study, I would put him through an exhausting walk before breakfast. The direction of all the nervous energies to the support of the muscular system, and the necessary draft upon the digestive and nutritive functions to supply the muscular waste, leave the mind temporarily a bankrupt. I have never seen a man who was really remarkable for acquired muscular power, and, at the same time, remarkable for mental power. A man may be born into the world with a fine muscular system and a fine brain, and in early life his muscular system may have a fine development. Such a man may subsequently have a remarkable mental development, but this development will never be accompanied by large and regular expenditures of muscular power. If I wished to repress the mental growth and manifestation of a man, I would undertake to educate him up to the point of lifting eight or ten kegs of nails. There is danger at first of overdoing our "muscular Christianity"—danger of getting more muscle than Christianity; and there is a good deal more danger of overdoing our muscular intellectuality. The difference between the kind and amount of exercise necessary to produce a healthy machine and the kind and amount necessary to produce a powerful one, is very great. We are never to look for great intellectuality in a professor of gymnastics, nor to expect that the time will come when a man will not only walk a thousand miles in a thousand hours, but compose a poem of a thousand lines at the same time.

If the temporary diversion of the nervous energy from the brain have this effect, what must a permanent diversion accomplish? It will accomplish precisely what is indicated by the look and language of our two young friends at the station-house. It will develop muscle for the uses of a special calling, and make ugly and clumsy men of those who should be symmetrical; and at the same time it will repress mental development, and permanently limit mental growth—at least, so long as the mind shall be associated with the body. I suppose that every fecundated germ of human being is endowed with a certain possibility of development—a complement of vital energy which will be expended in various directions, according to the circumstances which may surround it and the will of its possessor. If it shall be mainly expended upon the growth and sustentation of muscle, it will not be expended upon the growth and sustentation of mind; and I have no hesitation in saying that it is an absolute impossibility for a man who engages in hard bodily labor every day to be brilliant in intellectual manifestation. The tide of such a man's life does not set in that direction. An hour-glass has in it a definite quantity of sand; and when I turn it over, that sand falls from the upper apartment into the lower; and while it occupies that position it will continue to fall until the former is exhausted and the latter is filled. Moreover, it will never take its place at the other end of the instrument, until it is turned back. It is precisely thus with a human constitution. The grand vital current moves only in one direction, and when it is moving toward muscle it is not moving toward mind, and when it is moving toward mind it is not moving toward muscle. This fact is illustrated sufficiently by the phenomena of digestion. After a man has eaten a hearty dinner, he becomes dull, even to drowsiness or perfect sleep. Why? Simply because the tide of nervous energy sets towards digestion, and there is not enough left to carry on mental or voluntary muscular operations.

A resident of a city riding into the country, especially if he be an intellectual man, and engaged in intellectual pursuits, will be thrilled by what he sees around him. The life of the farmer, planted in the midst of so much that is beautiful, having to do with nature's marvellous miracles of germination and growth, moving under the open heaven with its glory of sky and meteoric change, and accompanied by the songs of birds and all characteristic rural sights and sounds, will seem to him the sweetest and the most enviable that falls to human lot. But the hard-working farmer sees nothing of this. What cares he for birds, unless they pull up his corn? What cares he for skies, unless he can make use of them for drying his hay, or wetting down his potatoes? The beautiful changes of nature do not touch him. His sensibilities are deadened by hard work. His nervous system is all imbedded in muscle, and does not lie near enough to the surface to be reached by the beauty and music around him. All he knows about a daisy is that it does not make good hay; and he draws no appreciable amount of the pleasure of his life from those surroundings which charm the sensibilities of others.

We are in the habit of regarding the farming population of the country as the most moral and religious of any, yet if we look at them critically, we shall find that their piety is of a negative, rather than a positive character. They are men in the first place who have very few temptations, either from without or from within. There are no professional tempters around them to lure them into the more seductive paths of sin. The woman whose steps take hold on hell does not pass their doors; the gambler spreads no snares for them; no gilded palace invites them to music and intoxicating draughts; they are not maddened by ambition; and they have no vanity that leads them to degrading and ruinous display. If they are little assailed from without, they are not more moved toward vice from within. The fact that their vital energies are all expended upon labor relieves them from the motives of temptation. Men whose muscles are overworked have no vitality to expend upon vices. The devil cannot make much out of a man who is both tired and sleepy. If we inquire of the ministers who have charge of rural parishes, they will usually tell us that an audience of mechanics is better than an audience of farmers, and that the miscellaneous audience of a city is better than either. It is impossible for men who have devoted every bodily energy they possess to hard labor during the waking hours of six days, to go to church and keep brightly awake on the seventh. Country ministers will also admit that they have in their parishes less help in social and conference meetings than the pastors of city parishes, and that no great movements of benevolence ever originate in, or are carried on by, rural churches.

As a matter of course, life cannot have much dignity or much that is characteristically human in it unless it be based upon active intellectuality, genuine sensibility, a development of the finer affections, and positive Christian virtue. When a man is a man, he never "tucks in grub." When a man lies down for rest and sleep he does not "go to roost." To a man, marriage is something more than "hitching on," and a dirty shirt is a good deal more of a "surprise" to a man's back than a clean one. There is no doubt about the fact that a life whose whole energies are expended in hard bodily labor is such a life as God never intended man should live. I do not wonder that men fly from this life and gather into the larger villages and cities, to get some employment which will leave them leisure for living. Life was intended to be so adjusted that the body should be the servant of the soul, and always subordinate to the soul. It was never meant by the Creator that the soul should always be subordinate to the body, or sacrificed to the body.

I am perfectly aware that I am not revealing pleasant truths. We are very much in the habit of glorifying rural life, and praising the intelligence and virtue of rural populations; and if they believe us, they cannot receive what I write upon this subject with pleasure. But the question which interests these people most is not whether my statements are pleasant but whether they are true. Is the philosophy sound? Are the facts as they are represented to be? Does a severe and constant tax upon the muscular system repress mental development, and tend to make life hard and homely and unattractive? Is this the kind of life generally which the American farmer leads? Is not the American farmer, generally, a man who has sacrificed a free and full mental development, and all his finer sensibilities and affections, and a generous and genial family and social life, and the dignities and tasteful proprieties of a well-appointed home, to the support of his muscles? I am aware that there are instances of a better life than this among the farmers, and I should not have written this article if those instances had not taught me that this everlasting devotion to labor is unnecessary. There are farmers who prosper in their calling, and do not become stolid. There are farmers who are gentlemen—men of intelligence—whose homes are the abodes of refinement, whose watchward is improvement, and whose aim it is to elevate their calling. If there be a man on the earth whom I honestly honor it is a farmer who has broken away from his slavery to labor, and applied his mind to his soil.

Mind must be the emancipator of the farmer. Science, intelligence, machinery—these must liberate the white bondman of the soil from his long slavery. When I look back and see what has been done for the farmer within my brief memory, I am full of hope for the future. The plough, under the hand of science, is become a new instrument. The horse now hoes the corn, digs the potatoes, mows the grass, rakes the hay, reaps the wheat, and threshes and winnows it; and every day adds new machinery to the farmer's stock, to supersede the clumsy implements which once bound him to his hard and never-ending toil. When a farmer begins to use machinery and to study the processes of other men, and to apply his mind to farming so far as he can make it take the place of muscle, then he illuminates his calling with a new light, and lifts himself into the dignity of a man. If mind once gets the upper hand, it will serve itself and see that the body is properly cared for. Intelligent farming is dignified living. For a farmer who reads and thinks, and studies and applies, nature will open the storehouse of her secrets, and point the way to a life full of dignity and beauty, and grateful and improvable leisure.

LESSON XIII.

REPOSE.

Peace, greatness best becomes; calm power doth guide
With a far more imperious stateliness
Than all the swords of violence can do,
And easier gains those ends she tends unto."

DANIEL.

When headstrong passion gets the reins of reason,
The force of nature, like too strong a gale,
For want of ballast oversets the vessel."

HIGGONS.

"Give me that man
That is not passion's slave, and I will wear him
In my heart's core, ay, in my heart of hearts,
As I do thee."

SHAKSPERE.

MRS. FLUTTER BUDGET was at church last Sunday. She always is at church; and she never forgets her fan. I have known her for many years, and have never known her to be in church without a fan in her hand, and some article upon her person that rustled constantly. Her black silk dress is death to devotion over the space of twenty feet on all sides of her. She fixes the wires in the bonnets of her little girls, then takes their hats off entirely, then wipes their noses, then shakes her head at them, then makes them exchange seats with each other, then finds the text and the hymns for them, then fusses with the cricket, and then fans herself unremittingly until she can see something else to do. During all this time, and throughout all these exercises, the one article of dress upon her fidgety person that has rustle in it, rustles. It chafes against the walls of silence as a caged bear chafes, with feverish restlessness, against the walls of his cell; and as if the annoyance of one sense were not sufficient, she seems to have adopted a bob-and-sinker style of trimming, for hat and dress, and hair and cloak, and every thing that goes to make up her externals. Little pendants are everywhere—little tassels, and little balls, and little tufts—at the end of little cords; and these are all the time bobbing up and down, and trembling, and threatening to bob up and down, like—

> "The one red leaf, the last of its clan
> That dances as often as dance it can,
> Hanging so light, and hanging so high,
> On the topmost bough that looks up at the sky."

Any person who sits near Mrs. Flutter Budget, or undertakes to look at her during divine service, loses all sense of repose, and all power of reflection. The most solemn exercises in which the mind engages cannot be carried on with a fly upon the nose, and any teasing of a single sense, whether of sight, or sound, or touch, is fatal to religious devotion. I presume that if the pastor wishes to find the most sterile portion of his field, he needs only to ascertain the names of those who occupy pews in the vicinity of this lively little lady. Her husband died two years ago, of sleeplessness, and a harassing system of nursing.

The Flutter Budgets are a numerous family in America. They are not all as restless as Madame, but the characteristics of the blood are manifest among them all. They never know repose; and, what is worse than this, they dread if they do not despise it. They are immense workers—not that they do more work, and harder than their neighbors, but they make a great fuss about it, and are always at it. They rise early in the morning, and they sit up late at night; and they do this from year's end to year's end, whether they really have any thing to do or not. They cannot sit still. They have an unhealthy impression that it is wrong for them not to be "doing something" all the time. Nothing in the world will make them so uncomfortable and so restless as leisure. Mrs. Flutter Budget could no more sit down without knitting-work, or a sock to darn, in her hands, than she could fly. As she has many times remarked, she would die if she could not work. To her, and to all of her name and character, constant action seems to be a necessity. The craving of the smoker for his pipe or cigar, the incessant hankering of the opium-eater for his drug, the terrible thirst of the drunkard for his cups—all these are legitimate illustrations of the morbid desire of the Budgets for action or motion. The man who has the habit of using narcotics is not more restless and unhappy without his accustomed stimulus, than they are with nothing to do. In truth, I believe the desire for action may become just as morbid a passion of the soul as that which most degrades and demoralizes mankind.

If I were called upon to define happiness, I could possibly give no definition that would shut out the word repose. I do not mean by this that no person can be happy except in a state of repose, but I mean, rather, that no man can be happy to whom repose is impossible. The highest definition of happiness would probably designate the consciousness of healthy powers harmoniously employed as among its prime elements; but there can be no happiness that deserves its name without the consciousness of powers that are able to subside from harmonious action into painless repose. I know a little girl who plays out of doors at night as long as she can see, and who, when called into the house, takes up a book with restless greed for mental excitement, and then begs to be read to sleep after she has been required to put down her book and go to bed. She would be called a happy child by those who see her playing among her mates, yet it is easy to perceive that her happiness is limited to a single attitude and condition of body and mind. A happier child than she is one who can enjoy open-air play, and then quietly sit down at her mother's side and enjoy rest. That is an inharmonious and unhealthy state of mind which chafes with leisure; and he is an unhappy man who cannot sit down for a moment without reaching for a newspaper, or looking about him for some quid for his morbid mind to chew upon. So I count no man truly happy who cannot contentedly sit still when circumstances release his powers from labor, and who does not reckon among the rewards of labor a peaceful repose.

No; Mrs. Flutter Budget is not a happy woman; and, as I have intimated before, she seriously interferes with the happiness and the spiritual prosperity of those about her. When she can find nothing to do, then she worries. Those children of hers are worried nearly to death. If, in their play, they get any dirt upon their faces, they are sent immediately to make themselves clean. If they soil their clothes, they are shut up until reduced to a proper state of penitence. They are kept out of all draughts of air for fear of a cold; and if they should take cold, why, they must take medicine of the most repulsive character as a penalty. If they cough out of the wrong corner of their mouths, she suspects them of croupy intentions; and if they venture, at some unguarded moment, on a cutaneous eruption, they are immediately charged with the measles, or accused of small-pox. If they quietly sit down for a moment of repose, she apprehends sickness, and stirs them about to shake it off. Even sleep is not sacred to her, for if she finds a flushed face among the harassed little slumberers, she wakes its owner to make affectionate inquiries. Her husband, as I have already stated, died two years ago. She worked upon his nervous system to such an extent that he was glad to be rid of the world, and of her. I think a man would die, after awhile, with constantly looking at the motion of a saw-mill. The jar of a locomotive makes the toughest iron brittle at last; and the wear and tear of a restless wife are beyond the strongest man's endurance.

I have noticed that persons who have influence upon the minds of others, maintain constantly a degree of repose. I do not mean that those have most influence who use their powers sparingly, but that a certain degree of mental repose—or what may possibly be called imperturbableness—is necessary to influence. Mrs. Flutter Budget always talks in a hurry, and talks of a thousand things, and is easily excited. Her neighbor, carefully avoiding the causes which ruffle her, and preserving the poise of her faculties, insists on her point quietly, and carries it. The repose of equanimity is a charm which dissolves all opposition. The mind which shows itself open to influences from every quarter, and is swayed by them, is not its own master. The mind that never rests is invariably full of freaks and caprices. The mind that has no repose shows its dependence and its lack of self-control. There cannot go out of such a mind as this a positive influence, any more than there can go forth from a candle a steady light, when it stands flickering and flaring in the wind, having all it can do to keep its flame from extinction. There must be that repose of mind which springs from conscious self-control and consciousness of the power of self-control, under all ordinary circumstances, before a man can hope to have influence of a powerful character upon the minds about him. The driver of a coach-and-six, with all the ribbons in his hands, and a thorough knowledge of his horses and his road, sits upon his box in repose; and that repose inspires me with confidence in him; but if he should be constantly on the look-out for some trick, and constantly examining his harnesses, and constantly fussy and uneasy, I should lose my confidence in him, and wish I were in anybody's care but his.

We do not need to be taught that a restless mind is not a reliable mind. There is an instinct which tells us this. There can be no reliableness of character without repose. If I should wish to take a ride, and two horses should be led before me to choose from, I would take the one that stands still, waiting for his burden and his command, rather than the one that occupies the road and his groom with his caracoling and curveting and other signs of restlessness. I should be measurably sure that one would bear me through my journey safely and speedily, and that the other would either throw me, or wear himself out, and so fail of giving me good service. Saint Peter was a restless man—an impatient man. He was always the most impulsive, and the most ready to act, as the servant of the high priest had occasion to remember; but he both lied and denied his Lord. It was John reposing upon the breast of Jesus, who most drew forth the Lord's affection. Martha, worrying about the house, cumbered with much serving, chose a part inferior to that of Mary who reposed at the feet of Jesus. It is only in repose that the powers of the mind are marshalled for great enterprises and for progress. It is in repose, when passion is sleeping and reason is clear-eyed, that the military chieftain marks out his campaign and arranges his forces. He is a poor commander who throws his troops into the field, and fights without order, or struggles for no definite end; and there are multitudes of men who throw themselves into life with an immense splutter, and fight the fight of life with a great deal of noise, but who never make any progress, because they have never drawn upon repose for a plan.

Repose is the cradle of power. It is the fashion to say that great men are men of great passions, as if their passions were the cause rather than the concomitant of their greatness. Great elephants have great legs, but the legs do not make the elephants great. Great legs, however, are required to move great elephants, and wherever we find great elephants, we find great legs. Small men sometimes have great passions, and these passions may so far overcome them that they shall be the weakest of the weak. The possession of great passions is often a disadvantage to weak men and strong men alike, because they furnish so many assailable points for outside forces. A fortress may be very strongly built, but if its doors are open, and scaling ladders are run permanently down from its walls for the accommodation of invading forces, its strength will be of very little practical advantage. Great passions are oftener the weak, than the strong points of great men. Now I do not believe it possible for a man to exercise a high degree of power upon the hearts and minds of others, and, at the same time, be under the influence of any variety of passion. A man cannot be the shivering subject of an outside force, acting upon him through his passions, and at the same time a centre of effluent power. Action and passion are opposed to each other; and when one has possession of the soul the other is wanting. They involve two distinct attitudes of the mind, as truly as do thanksgiving and petition.

The world often finds fault with great men because they are cold; but they could not be great men if they were not cold. A physician is often preferred by a family or patient because he is "so sympathizing," as they call it. They forget that a physician is necessarily untrustworthy in the degree that he is sympathetic with his patients. A physician may be thoroughly kind, and out of his kindness there may grow a gentle manner which seems to spring from sympathy; but I say unhesitatingly that in the degree by which a physician is sympathetic with his patients, is he unfitted for his work. A dentist who feels, in sympathy, the pain that he inflicts upon a child, is unfitted to perform his operation. The surgeon who sensitively sympathizes with a man whose diseased or crushed limb it has fallen to his lot to remove, has lost a portion of his power and skill, and has become a poorer surgeon for his sympathy. Physicians themselves show that they understood this when a case for medical or surgical treatment occurs in their own families. If their wives or their children are sick, they cannot control their sympathies; and the moment they are aware of this, they lose all confidence in themselves. They cannot reduce the fracture of a child's limb, or prescribe for a wife lying dangerously ill, because their sympathies are so greatly excited that their judgment is good for nothing. In other words, they are in an attitude or condition of passion—they are moved and wrought upon by outside forces, to such a degree that they cannot act.

If an orator rise in his place, and show by the agitation of his nerves, his broken sentences, and his choked utterances, that emotion is uppermost in him, he has no more power upon his audience than a baby. We pity his weakness, or we sympathize with him; but he cannot move us. He is a mastered man, and until he can choke down his passion he cannot master us. A man rises in an audience in a state of furious excitement, and fumes, and yells, and gesticulates, but he only moves us to pity, or disgust, or laughter. His passion utterly deprives him of power. We call Mr. Gough an actor, as he undoubtedly is; and we pretend to be disgusted with him for simulating every night, for a hundred nights in succession, the emotions which move us. We forget that if Mr. Gough should really become the subject of the passions which he illustrates, he would lose his power upon us, and kill himself besides. He takes care never to be mastered, and takes care also that all the machinery which he uses shall contribute to his mastery of us. I do not deny that passion may be made tributary to the power of men. Oil is tributary to the power of machinery by lubricating its points of friction; and warmth, by bringing its members into more perfect adjustment; but if the machinery were made to wade in oil, or were heated red hot, oil and heat would be a damage to it.

I repeat the proposition, then, that repose is the cradle of power. The man who cannot hold his passions in repose—in perfect repose—can never employ the measure of his power. These "cold men," as the world calls them, are the men who move and control their race. But it is not necessary to cling to great men for the illustration of my subject. To say that a Christian philanthropist should not be a sympathetic man would be to say that he should not be a man at all; but nothing is more certain than that if a man should surrender himself to his sympathies it would kill him. In a world where sin and its bitter fruits abound as they do in this, where little children cry for bread, and whole races are sunk in barbarism, and villainy preys upon virtue, and the innocent suffer in the place of the guilty, and sickness lays its hand upon multitudes, and pain holds its victims to a life-long bondage, and death leads throngs daily to the grave, and leaves other throngs wild with grief, a sensitively sympathetic man, surrendering himself to all the influences that address him, would lose all power to help the distressed, or even to speak a word of comfort. We are to apprehend the woes of others through our sympathies, and to hold those sympathies in such repose that all the power of our natures will be held ready for, and subject to, intelligent ministry. The woman who faints at the sight of blood is not fit for a hospital. The man who grows pale at hearing a groan, will not do for a surgeon. If we mean to do any thing in this world for the good of men, we must first compel our sympathies and our passions into repose.

That which is true of power in this matter is true of judgment. It is a widely bruited aphorism that "all history is a lie," and this aphorism had its birth in the fact that historians become, as it were, magnetized by the characters with which they deal. A man who writes the life of Napoleon finds himself either sympathizing with him, or roused into antipathy by him. In short, he becomes the subject of a passion, wrought upon him by the character which he contemplates and undertakes to paint; and from the moment this passion takes possession of him, he becomes unfitted to write an impartial and reliable word about him. All positive historical characters have all possible historical portraits, simply because the writers are subjects of passion. It is because no man can write of positive characters without being the subject of an influence from them, that no man can be an impartial historian, and that all history must necessarily be a lie. If ever a perfect history shall be written, it will be written by one whose passions are under entire control, and kept in a condition of profound repose—who will look at a historical character as he would upon an impaled beetle in an entomological collection. A man is no competent judge of a character, either in history or in life, with which he strongly sympathizes. I have known many a man utterly unfitted to read the proofs of the villainy of one to whom he had surrendered his sympathies. A woman in love is a very poor judge of character. She can see nothing but excellence where others see nothing but shallowness and rottenness.

Once more, there is no dignity without repose. A restless, uneasy man, can never be a dignified man. There can be no dignity about a man or a woman who fumes, and frets, and fusses, and is full of freaks and caprices. Dignity of manners is always associated with repose. Mrs. Flutter Budget always enters a drawing-room as if she were a loaded doll, tossed in by the usher, and goes dodging and tipping about to get her centre of gravity, without getting it. Her queenly neighbor comes in as the sun rises—calmly, sweetly, steadily, and all hearts bow to her dignified coming. What would an Archbishop be worth for dignity, who should be continually scratching his ears, and brushing his nose, and crossing and re-crossing his legs, and drumming with his fingers? Who would not deem the ermine degraded by a chief justice who should be constantly twitching about upon his bench? It is a fact that has come under the observation of the least observant, that the moment a man surrenders himself to his passions he loses his dignity. A fit of anger is as fatal to dignity as a dose of arsenic to life. A fit of mirthfulness is hardly less fatal. So it is in repose, and particularly in the repose of the passions, that we find the happiness, the influence, the power, and the dignity of our life. Let us cultivate repose.

LESSON XIV.

THE WAYS OF CHARITY.

"The Holy Supper is kept indeed,
In whatso we share with another's need;
Not that which we give, but what we share,
For the gift without the giver is bare:
Who bestows himself, with his alms feeds three,—
Himself, his hungering neighbor, and me."

LOWELL.

"It may not be our lot to wield
The sickle in the ripened field;
Nor ours to hear on summer eves,
The reaper's song among the sheaves;
Yet, when our duty's task is wrought,
In unison with God's great thought,
The near and future blend in one,
And whatsoe'er is willed is done."

WHITTIER.

I HAVE come to entertain very serious doubts about my "orthodoxy" on the subject of doing good. If I know my own motives, I certainly have a desire to do good; but this desire is yoke fellow with the perverse wish to do it in my own way. I do not feel myself inclined to accept the prescriptions of those who have taken out patents for various ingenious processes in this line of effort. My attention has just been attracted to this subject, by the perusal of a long story, which must be not far from the one hundred and ninety-ninth that I have read during the past twenty years, all tipped with the same general moral. A good-natured lady, in easy circumstances, and of benevolent impulses, is appealed to by a poor man in the kitchen. She feeds him, gives him clothes, sends him away rejoicing, and feels good over it. The man comes again and again, tells pitiful stories, excites her benevolence of course, and secures a reasonable amount of additional plunder. Months pass away; and being out upon a walk one pleasant afternoon, and finding herself near the poor man's residence, the fair benefactress calls upon him. She finds the wife (who was reported dead) very comfortable indeed, and the destitute family of four children reduced to a single fat and saucy baby, and the poor liar himself smelling strongly of rum. Then come the denouement, and a grand tableau: lady very much grieved and astonished—wife, who has known nothing of her husband's tricks, exceedingly bewildered—fuddled husband, blind with rum and remorse, owns up to his meanness and duplicity. He found (as he confessed) that he could work upon the lady's sympathies, got to lying and couldn't stop, and, finally, felt so badly over the whole operation, that he took to drink to drown his conscience! *Moral:* Women should not help poor people without going to see them, and finding out whether they lie.

Now that woman did exactly as I should have done, under the same circumstances. In the first place, I should never have had the heart to doubt a man who carried an honest face, and was cold, hungry, and ragged. I should have regarded his condition as a claim upon my charity. In the second place, I should have had no time to call upon his family, and satisfy myself with regard to their circumstances; and in the third place, I should have felt very delicate about putting direct questions to them if I had. The same story tells incidentally of one of these men who do good in the proper way. He visited a house which presented all the signs of poverty; but the angel of mercy was too 'cute to be taken in; so he walked up stairs. Every thing presenting there the same aspect of abject poverty that prevailed below, the angel of mercy looked around him, and discovered a ladder leading to the garret. The angel of mercy "smelt a rat," and mounted the ladder. In the garret he found half a cord of wood, and any quantity of goodies for the table. Another denouement and tableau. *Moral:* as before. If the story has taught me any thing, it is that it is my duty to question every beggar that comes to my door, visit his house, explore it from cellar to garret, and satisfy myself of the truth or falsehood of his representations. Otherwise, my charity goes for nothing, and I do my beggar an absolute unkindness. In other words, while the law holds every man innocent until he is proved to be guilty, charity holds every man guilty until he is proved to be innocent.

It has become the fashion in certain circles to decry that benevolence which sits at home in slippers, and gives its money without seeing where it goes; but it is forgotten that the money dispensed in slippers was earned in boots, and that the man who has money to give, has usually so much business on hand that he can make no adequate personal examination of the cases which are referred to his charity. I can never forget Mr. Dickens' Cheeryble Brothers, who were so very much obliged to a friend for calling upon them, and telling them of the circumstances of a poor family. It was taken as a great personal kindness when they were informed how and where they could relieve want and distress. They had no genius for going about and looking up cases of charity, but their hearts leaped at the opportunity to do good. They did their work in their counting-room, and had no time and no talent for visiting those whom they benefited; but who would question either the genuineness or the judiciousness of their benevolence? The applications for aid made at the doors of our dwellings come oftener to the mistresses of those dwellings than to the masters; and these mistresses, four times in five, are women with the care of children on their hands, or household duties which demand almost constant attention. If a beggar come to the door, they are grateful for the opportunity to afford relief; but they have no time to visit another quarter of the town, to learn whether their charities have been well bestowed, nor do they withhold their charities through fear of being imposed upon.

In my judgment, the character and circumstances of a man determine his office in the work of charitable relief. I know there are some persons who have a peculiar natural adaptation to the work of visiting the subjects of sickness and of need. Their presence and their sympathy are grateful to those to whom they delight to minister. They are masters and mistresses of all those thrifty economies which enable them to manage for the poor. They have genuine administrative talent in this particular department. They are cheerful and active, and sympathetic and ingenious; and they can do more for a poor, discouraged family with ten dollars than others can do with fifty. I do not suppose that these people are one whit more benevolent than those whose purses are always open to the poor, and who at the same time would feel very awkward upon a visit of charity, and would make the family visited feel as awkward as themselves. The poor we have always with us; and every man and woman who possesses means for their relief owes a duty to them which is to be discharged in the most efficient way. If I have money, and do not feel that I am the proper person to look after the details of its dispensation, I will put it into the hands of one more competent to the business, and I will rationally conclude that I have done my duty. In the mean time, if a man come to my door, and ask for the supply of his immediate necessities, he shall not be turned empty away because I do not happen to have the means at hand for verifying his story.

I know that there are multitudes of tender-hearted women—women of abounding benevolence and sensitive conscience—who are troubled upon this subject. They have a desire to do good, and to do it in the right way; but, somehow, they find it impossible to do it according to the views of the story-writers. They are any thing but rugged in health, perhaps, or they have a dependent family of young children around them, or the care of their dwellings absorbs their time. They fail to find the opportunity to visit the poor, or they do not feel themselves adapted to the office; and still they carry about with them the uncomfortable suspicion that they are meanly shrinking from duty. My thought upon this point is that my duties never conflict with one another, and that if I can do good in one way better than another, then that is my way to do good. I shall not permit the story-writers to prescribe for me, nor shall I allow them to make me uncomfortable.

There is a class of men and women in all Protestant communities who think it a very neat thing to do good at random. They sow broadcast of cheap seed, content to reap nothing at all, and pleasantly disappointed if they find here and there a stalk of corn to reward their sowing. They do not prepare their ground, they do not cultivate it at all, but they sow, hoping that in some open place a seed may fall and germinate. Some of these people regard this method of doing good as a kind of holy stratagem—a Christian trick—which takes the devil at a disadvantage. I once knew a kind old gentleman who did a business that brought him considerably into contact with rough and profane persons; and as he wished to do something for them, he kept his pockets filled with little printed cards entitled "The Swearer's Prayer;" and whenever an oath came out, the utterer was immediately presented with this card with a little story on it, and a statement that "to swear is neither brave, polite, nor wise." I very well remember hearing the old gentleman say that, though he had given away hundreds of these cards, he had never learned that one of them had done any good. I do not wonder at it. It was a sneaking way of doing good, or of trying to. If the old man had remonstrated personally with these swearing fellows, and told them that their habit was both vulgar and wicked, does any one suppose that the result would have been so unsatisfactory? He had not pluck enough to do this; so he gave them a card, and they either threw it in his face or threw it away. But then, the cards didn't cost much!

I have been much interested in watching a car-load of passengers, while receiving each from the hands of a professional distributor a religious tract. All have received the gift politely, in deference to the motive which prompted, or was supposed to prompt, its bestowal; yet I have never failed to perceive that politeness was really taxed in the matter. Now let me be candid, and confess that I was never pleasantly impressed by being presented with a tract in a railroad car. This fact cannot be attributed to any lack of disposition to contemplate religious subjects; but there is something which tells me that it is improper and indelicate for any man to come into a public vehicle, and thrust upon me and upon my fellow-passengers a set of motives and opinions on religion which may or may not accord with my own and theirs—just as it happens. I think the natural action of the mind is to brace itself against influences sought to be sprung upon it in this manner; and I am yet to be convinced that this indiscriminate and wholesale distribution of religious tracts in railroad stations and public conveyances is not doing, and has not done, more harm than good. I know that multitudes of men—not vicious—are disgusted with it, and offended by it, and that there is something—call it what you may—in the emotions excited by the presentation of a tract under such ill-chosen circumstances, which counteracts any good influence it was intended to produce. A gentleman will receive a tract politely, and read it or not according to his whim; but it will be very apt to disgust him with the style of Christianity which it represents.

I am aware that the secretary and the agents of the tract societies make very encouraging reports of the results of their operations. I am always interested in these details, and do not discredit at all the statements which they make. Nay, I am convinced that in certain departments of their effort they are successful in doing much good. I believe that their noble army of colporteurs, going from lonely neighborhood to neighborhood, and carrying with them an unselfish, devoted life, and the living voice of prayer, exhortation, and counsel, win many souls to Christian virtue. I am willing to acknowledge, further, that here and there a tract, chance-sown, may fall into ground ready to receive it; but I have a right to question whether the same outlay of effort and money, applied directly in other fields, would not bring very much larger returns. My point is that in all efforts to do good, in this way, appropriateness of time and place is always to be consulted. I once took my seat in a dentist's chair to have an operation performed upon my teeth. If I remember correctly, an ugly fang was to be removed,—at any rate, pain was involved in the matter; but no sooner was the dentist's arm around my head, and his instrument in my mouth, than the well-meaning and zealous operator began to question me upon the subject of personal religion. Now it seemed quite as bad to undertake to propagate Christianity at the point of a surgical instrument, as it would be to win proselytes by the sword; and the utter incongruity of the two operations disgusted me. At any rate, *I changed my dentist.* I felt like the man who found upon his landlady's table an article of butter that was inconveniently encumbered with hair, and who informed her that he had no objection to hair, but would prefer to have it served upon a separate dish.

A good many years ago, I read a Sunday-school book entitled, if I remember correctly, "Walks of Usefulness." It represented a man going out into the street, and "pitching into" every person he met with, upon the subject of religion, or starting a conversation and immediately giving it a spiritual twist. I thought then that he was a remarkably ingenious man—a wonderful story-teller, to say the least of him. I am inclined to think now that he romanced a little. Every operation was so neatly done, and turned out so well, that I really suspect it was pure fiction. I have this to say, at any rate, that if he did and said what he professed to have done and said, under the circumstances which he described, he owed it to the politeness of those whom he addressed that he was not dismissed with a decided rebuff, and told to go about his business. "A word fitly spoken, how good it is!" Ah yes! how very good it is! Christian zeal is no excuse for bad taste, nor is Christian effort exempt from the laws of fitness and propriety which attach to human effort of other aims in other fields. If I wish to reach a man's mind upon any important subject, and circumstances do not favor me, I wait for circumstances to change, or I pave my way to his mind by a series of carefully-adjusted efforts. Abrupt transitions of thought and feeling, and violent interruptions of the currents of mental life and action, are never favorable to reflection. If I wish to cheer a man who is bowed to the earth in grief for the loss of a companion, I will not break in upon his mourning with a lively tune upon a fiddle. If I wish to attract him to a religious life, I will not interrupt the flow of his innocently social hours by some terrible threat or warning. In truth, I know of nothing that calls for more care, or nicer discrimination, or choicer address, than a personal attempt to move an irreligious mind in a religious direction. The word of gold should always have a setting of silver.

There seems to be a prevalent disposition in the religious world to do good by indirection and stratagem. If a man can reach one mind by scattering ten thousand tracts, the result is more grateful than it would be if that mind were reached by direct personal effort without any tracts; and it makes a larger and more interesting show in the reports. This disposition is manifest in the matter of charitable fairs. The women of a religious society will make up a batch of little-or-nothings, freeze a few cans of ice cream, hire a hall, and advertise a sale. We all go, and buy things that we do not want, with a good-natured and gallant disregard of prices, and the footings of receipts are published in the newspapers. The charitable women feel pleasantly about it, and think that they have done a great deal of good at a small cost, without remembering that all the money they have made has cost somebody the amount of the declared figures. It seems to be a great deal pleasanter to get possession of the money in this way, than it would be to obtain it by a general subscription. They forget that all they have done is to obtain a subscription by a graceful and attractive stratagem, and that the motives which they have pocketed with the money would not stand the test of a scrupulous analysis. The main point seems to be to get the money, and do the good with the least possible sense of sacrifice; as a man goes to a charitable ball, and pays two dollars for the privilege of dancing all night, in order to give a shilling of profits to the widow and fatherless without feeling the burden of the charity.

Of all the means of doing good, I know of none so repulsive as that which is purely professional. I think we do not have so much of this in these days as our fathers had. Our pastors are more thoroughly our companions and friends than they used to be. They do not assume to be our dictators and censors as they did in the earlier days of Puritanism. The idea of the regular parochial visit is essentially changed. But I know clergymen, even now, who visit the house of mourning professionally, and give their professional consolation in a professional way, and depart feeling that they have faithfully performed their professional duty. I know clergymen who go round from house to house with their professional inquiries, and do up any quantity of professional work in a day. The family come in, (those who do not run away,) and take seats around the room, and answer questions, and listen to a prayer, and then they bid their pastor a good afternoon with a sense of relief, and go about their business again, while he pushes on to his next parishioner, and repeats the professional task. It is all a dry and unfruitful formality on the part of the families visited, and a professionally-discharged duty on the part of the pastor, and a pitifully-ridiculous caricature of the visit of a religious teacher to his disciples every way. What shall be said of an interview of which the pastor's part consisted of these words: "Very late spring—Hem!" (looking out of the window)—"who is building that barn?—potatoes seem to be getting along very well;" (turning to a member of the family)—"Jane, how do you enjoy your mind?" A spiritual frame that could stand such a transition as that, without taking a fatal cold, must be based upon a very sound constitution, and toughened by frequent repetition of the process.

I suppose there will always be obtuse men in the pastoral office—men who know no way of getting into a sensitive soul except by knocking in the door and walking in with their boots on; but all such men are out of their place. The souls of an average people—tied to the tasks of life, burdened by care, oppressed by routine, and depressed in many instances by bodily weakness—need sympathy more than counsel, and encouragement and inspiration more than a solemn, professional catechetical probing of their religious state. But I think, as I have already said, that the world is improving in this matter. Our pastors are more social, more facile, more appreciative of the fact that, in all their personal intercourse with their people, they must win love and give sympathy if they would do good in the line of their profession.

So much in the vein of criticism; and if I am asked what guide a man shall have in the matter of doing good in the world, I shall answer: a loving, honest, and brave heart, and a mind that judges for itself. The heart that loves its fellow-men will move its possessor to do good; and the mind that thinks and judges for itself will decide in what direction its efforts ought to be made. If a man be moved to do good, he will do it, and his heart will lead him in the right direction. Under a mistaken sense of duty, inculcated by incompetent counsellors, men find themselves in fields of benevolent action to which they are very poorly adapted; and the world is full of these blunders; but an honestly-loving heart and an ordinarily clear brain, that nobody has been allowed to meddle with and muddle, will tell a man where he belongs and what he ought to do. If a man have a gift for ministering to the sick, let him do it. If he have a gift for dealing personally with the poor, let him do that. If he have a gift for making money, and none for properly applying his charities, let him hand his money to those who are competent to dispense it. I do not believe that many loving hearts, coupled with unsophisticated judgments, are engaged in indiscriminate and random efforts to act for religious ends upon the minds they meet with. I believe that with all such hearts and judgments there is connected a sense of that which is fit and proper in time, place, and circumstance, so that wherever they strike they leave their mark. I believe that such hearts and judgments will scorn to do that by indirection which they can do better directly, and that if it be fit and proper for them to offer reproof to a man, they will do it by the brave word of mouth, and not sneak up to him and put a card or a tract into his hand. I believe that men with such hearts and judgments would prefer making a subscription directly to a charitable object, to making one indirectly by paying double price for articles they do not want. And last, I think that pastors, with such hearts and judgments, are not at all in danger of becoming coldly professional in their noble duties. A life in any sphere that is the expression and outflow of an honest, earnest, loving heart, taking counsel only of God and itself, will be certain to be a life of beneficence in the best possible direction.

LESSON XV.

MEN OF ONE IDEA.

"Cultivate the physical exclusively, and you have an athlete or a savage; the moral only, and you have an enthusiast or a maniac; the intellectual only, and you have a diseased oddity—it may be a monster. It is only by wisely training all three together that the complete man can be formed."

SAMUEL SMILES.

WHEN the heats of summer have dried up the streams, and cataracts only trickle and drip, and the dams of brooks and rivers cease to pour the arching crystal from their lips, I have always loved to explore the forsaken water-courses. An imprisoned fish, a shell with rainbow lining, a curiously-worn rock, a strangely-tinted and grotesquely-fashioned stone—these are always objects of interest. Then to sit down upon a ledge that has been planed off by ice, and smoothed by the tenuous passage of an ocean's palpitating volume, and watch the shrunken stream slipping around its feet, and hear the gurgle of the faintly-going water, and grow so drowsy with the song that it breaks at last into surprising articulations, and talks and laughs, and shouts and sings—ah! this, indeed, is enchantment! There are few men, I suppose, so fortunate as to have enjoyed a country breeding, who do not recall scenes like this,—who do not remember a half-holiday, at least, spent in the bed of a summer stream, and at the feet of scanty cataracts, making fierce attacks on water snakes, watching lizards lying among the stones of an old raceway, creeping up, hat in hand, to a gauze-winged devil's needle that shivered on a sunny point of rock, and looked as if it might be the ghost of a humming-bird, starting to mark the sudden flight and hear the chattering cry of the king-fisher as he darted through the shadows and disappeared, and noting the slim-legged wagtail, racing backward and forward upon the border of the stream.

Among the objects of interest very often, if not always, to be found at the feet of dams and cataracts, are what people call "pot-holes." They are round holes worn in the solid rock by a single stone, kept in motion by the water. Some of them are very large and others are small. When the stream becomes dry, there they are, smooth as if turned out by machinery, and the hard, round pebbles at the bottom by which the curious work was done. Every year, as the dry season comes along, we find that the holes have grown larger and the pebbles smaller, and that no freshet has been found powerful enough to dislodge the pebbles and release the rock from their attrition. Now if a man will turn from the contemplation of one of these pot-holes, and the means by which it is made, and seek for that result and that process in the world of mind which most resemble them, I am sure that he will find them in a man of one idea. In truth, these scenes that I have been painting were all recalled to me by looking upon one of these men, studying his character, and watching the effect of the single idea by which he was actuated. "There," said I, involuntarily, "is a moral pot-hole with a pebble in it; and the hole grows larger and the pebble smaller every year."

I suppose it is useless to undertake to reform men of one idea. The real trouble is that the pebble is in them; and whole freshets of truth are poured upon them, only with the effect to make it more lively in its grinding, and more certain in its process of wearing out itself and them. The little man who, when ordered by his physician to take a quart of medicine, informed him with a deprecatory whimper that he did not hold but a pint, illustrates the capacity of many of those who are subjects of a single idea. They do not hold but one, and it would be useless to prescribe a larger number. In a country like ours, in which every thing is new and everybody is free, there are multitudes of self-constituted doctors, each of whom has a nostrum for curing all physical and moral disorders and diseases,—a patent process by which humanity may achieve its proudest progress and its everlasting happiness. The country is full of hobby-riders, booted and spurred, who imagine they are leading a grand race to a golden goal, forgetful of the truth that their steeds are tethered to a single idea, around which they are revolving only to tread down the grass and wind themselves up, where they may stand at last amid the world's ridicule, and starve to death.

Man cannot live by bread alone, but by every word that proceeds out of the mouth of God, whether spoken through nature or revelation. There is no one idea in all God's universe so great and so nutritious that it can furnish food for an immortal soul. Variety of nutriment is absolutely essential, even to physical health. There are so many elements that enter into the structure of the human body, and such variety of stimuli requisite for the play of its vital forces, that it is necessary to lay under tribute a wide range of nature; and fruits and roots and grain, beasts of the field, fowls of the air, and fish of the sea, juices and spices and flavors, all bring their contributions to the perfection of the human animal, and the harmony of its functions. The sailor, kept too long upon his hard biscuit and salt junk, degenerates into scurvy. The occupant of the Irish hovel who lives upon his favorite root, and sees neither bread nor meat, grows up with weak eyes, an ugly face, and a stunted body. It is precisely thus with a man who occupies and feeds his mind with a single idea. He grows mean and small and diseased with the diet. The soul bears relation to such a wealth of truth, such a multitude of interests cluster about it, it has such variety of elements—as illustrated by its illimitable range of action and passion—it touches and receives impressions from all other souls at such an infinite variety of points, that it is simply absurd to suppose that one idea can feed it, even for a day.

A mind that surrenders itself to a single idea becomes essentially insane. I know a man who has dwelt so long upon the subject of a vegetable diet that it has finally taken possession of him. It is now of such importance in his eyes that every other subject is thrown out of its legitimate relations to him. It is the constant theme of his thought—the study of his life. He questions the properties and quantities of every mouthful that passes his lips, and watches its effects upon him. He reads upon this subject every thing he can lay his hands on. He talks upon it with every man he meets. He has ransacked the whole Bible for support to his theories; and the man really believes that the eternal salvation of the human race hinges upon a change of diet. It has become a standard by which to decide the validity of all other truth. If he did not believe that the Bible was on his side of the question, he would discard the Bible. Experiments or opinions that make against his faith are either contemptuously rejected or ingeniously explained away. Now this man's mind is not only reduced to the size of his idea, and assimilated to its character, but it has lost its soundness. His reason is disordered. His judgment is perverted—depraved. He sees things in unjust and illegitimate relations. The subject that absorbs him has grown out of proper proportions, and all other subjects have shrunk away from it. I know another man—a man of fine powers—who is just as much absorbed by the subject of ventilation; and though both of these men are regarded by the community as of sound mind, I think they are demonstrably insane.

If we rise into larger fields, we shall find more notable demonstration of the starving effect of the entertainment of a single idea. Scattered throughout the country we shall find men who have devoted themselves to the cause of temperance, or abstinence from intoxicating liquors. Here is a grand, a humane, a most worthy and important cause; yet temperance as an idea is not enough to furnish food for a human soul. Some of these men have only room in them for one idea, and, so far as they are concerned, it might as well be temperance as any thing, though it is bad for the cause; but the majority of them were, at starting, men of generous instincts, a quick sense of that which is pure and true, and a genuine love of mankind. They dwelt upon their idea—they lived upon it for a few years—and then they "showed their keeping." If I should wish to find a narrow-minded, uncharitable, bigoted soul, in the smallest possible space of time, I would look among those who have made temperance the specialty of their lives—not because temperance is bad, but because one idea is bad; and the men afflicted by this particular idea are numerous and notorious. They have no faith in any man who does not believe exactly as they do. They accuse every man of unworthy motives who opposes them. They permit no liberty of individual judgment and no range of opinion; and when they get a chance, they drive legislation into the most absurd and harmful extremes. Men of one idea are always extremists, and extremists are always nuisances. I might truthfully add that an extremist is never a man of sound mind.

The whole tribe of professional agitators and miscalled reformers are men of one idea. That these men do good, sometimes directly and frequently indirectly, I do not deny; and it is equally evident that they do a great deal of harm, the worst of which, perhaps, falls upon themselves. Like the charge of a cannon, they do damage to an enemy's fortifications, but they burn up the powder there is in them, and lose the ball. Like blind old Samson, they may prostrate the pillars of a great wrong, but they crush themselves and the Philistines together. The greatest and truest reformer that ever lived was Jesus Christ; but ah! the difference between his broad aims, universal sympathies, and overflowing love, and the malignant spirit that moves those who angrily beat themselves to death against an instituted wrong! As an illustration, look at those who have been the prominent agitators of the slavery question in this country for the last twenty years. Are they men of charity? Are they Christian men? Is not invective the chosen and accustomed language of their lips? Do they not follow those against whom they have opposed themselves, whether for good cause or otherwise, into their graves with a fiendish lust of cruelty, and do they not delight to trample upon great names and sacred memories? Are they men whom we love? Do we feel attracted to their society? Teachers of toleration, are they not the most intolerant of all men living? Denouncers of bigotry, are they not the most fiercely bigoted of any men we know? Preachers of love and good will to men, do they not use more forcibly than any other class the power of words to wound and poison human sensibilities?

It is not the quality of the idea which a man entertains that kills him. Freedom for every creature that bears God's image—the breaking of the rod of the oppressor and letting the oppressed go free—this is a good idea. It is so great, so broad, so full, so flowing, that a world of men might gather around it for a time as they do around Niagara, and grow divine in its majestic music and the vision of the wreath of light which heaven holds above it. If a man undertake to live upon a single idea, it really makes very little difference to him whether that idea be a good or a bad one. A man may as well get scurvy on beans as beef. I suppose a diet of potatoes would be quite as likely to support life comfortably as a diet of peaches. It is because the human soul cannot live upon one thing alone, but demands participation in every expression of the life of God, that it will dwarf and starve upon even the grandest and most divine idea.

The agitators and reformers are very ready to see the dwarfing effect of a single idea or a single range of ideas upon the Christian ministry, and a large number of Christian men. I admit the accuracy of their observations in this matter, and, admitting this, I can certainly ask the question whether they hope to escape depreciation when the Christian idea—the divinest of all—is insufficient of itself to make a man, and fill him, and give him all desirable health and wealth and growth. As I have touched upon this point, I may say that it is coming to be understood that a man or a minister, in order to be a Christian, must be something else—that Christianity received into nature and life is only one of the elements of manhood—and that a man may become starved and mean and bigoted and essentially insane by feeding exclusively upon religion. What means the vision of these sapless, sad, and sanctimonious Christians—these poor, thin, stingy lives—but that all ideas save the religious one have been shut out from them? Is it not notorious that a minister who has fed exclusively upon religion is a man without power upon the hearts and minds of men? Is it not true that he has most efficiency in pulpit ministration who has the largest knowledge of and sympathy with men, the broadest culture, and the widest acquaintance with all the ideas that enter as food and motive into human life? Is it not true that in the life-long, absorbing anxiety and carefulness of a multitude of souls to secure their salvation, those souls are constantly becoming less valuable, and thus—to use the language of the market—less worth saving?

I cannot fail, however unwilling, to see much that is dry and stiff and unlovely in the style of Christianity around me. It has no attraction for me. I do not like the people who illustrate it; and the reason is, not that they have got too much of Christianity, but that they have not got enough of any thing else. Flour is good, but flour is not bread. If I am to eat flour, I must eat it as bread; and either milk or water must be used to make it bread. If a little milk is used, the bread will be dry and heavy and hard. If a good deal is used, the flour will be transformed into a soft and plastic mass, which will rise in the heat, and come to my lips a sweet and fragrant morsel. Christianity is good, but it wants mixing with humanity before it will have a practical value. If only a little humanity be mixed with it, the product will be dry and tasteless; but if it be combined with the real milk of humanity, and enough of it, the result will be a loaf fit for the tongues of angels. No: the divinest idea that has yet been apprehended by the human mind is not enough for the human mind. That which God made to be fed by various food cannot be fed with success or safety by a single element. We cannot build a house of dry bricks. It takes lime and sand and water in their proper proportions to hold the bricks together.

This selection of a single idea from the great world of ideas to which the mind is vitally related, and making it food and drink, and motive and pivotal point of action, and supreme object of devotion, is mental and moral suicide. It makes that a despotic king which should be a tributary subject. It enslaves the soul to a base partisanship. It is right to make money, and it is right to be rich when wealth is won legitimately; but when money becomes the supreme object of a man's life, the soul starves as rapidly as the coffers are filled. It is right to be a temperance man and an anti-slavery man, and an advocate of any special Christian reform; but the effect of adopting any one of these reforms as the supreme object of a man's pursuit, never fails to belittle him. One of the most pitiable objects the world contains is a man of generous natural impulses grown sour, impatient, bitter, abusive, uncharitable, and ungracious, by devotion to one idea, and the failure to impress it upon the world with the strength by which it possesses himself. Many of these fondly hug the delusion to themselves that they are martyrs, when, in fact, they are only suicides. Many of these look forward to the day when posterity will canonize them, and lift them to the glory of those who were not received by their age because they were in advance of their age. So they regard with contempt the pigmy world, wrap the mantles of their mortified pride about them, and lie down in a delusive dream of immortality.

Whether the effect of devotion to a single idea be disastrous or otherwise to the devotees, nothing in all history is better proved—nothing in all philosophy is more clearly demonstrable—than the fact that it is a damage to the idea. If I wished to disgust a community with any special idea, I would set a man talking about it and advocating it who would talk of nothing else. If I wished to ruin a cause utterly, I would submit it to the advocacy of one who would thrust it into every man's face, who would make every other cause subordinate to it, who would refuse to see any objections to it, who would accuse all opponents of unworthy motives, and who would thus exhibit his absolute slavery to it. Men have an instinct which tells them that such people as these are not trustworthy—that their sentiments and opinions are as valueless as those of children. If they talk with a pleasant spirit, we good-naturedly tolerate them; if they rant and scold and denounce, we hiss them if we think it worth while, or we applaud them as we would the feats of a dancing bear. If they say devilish things in a heavenly sort of way, and clothe their black malignities in silken phrases, we hear them with a certain kind of pleasure, and take our revenge in despising them, and feeling malicious towards the cause they advocate. It would kill us to drink Cologne water, but the perfume titillates the sense, and so we sprinkle it upon our handkerchiefs.

No great cause can be forwarded by the advocacy of men who have no character, and no man can devote himself to an idea without the loss of character. When a man comes forward to promulgate an idea, we inquire into his credentials. How large a man is this? How broad are his sympathies? How wide is his knowledge? What relation does he bear to the great world of ideas among which this is only one, and very likely a comparatively unimportant one? Is he so weak as to be possessed by this idea, or does he possess it, and entertain a rational comprehension of its relations to himself and the community? I know that multitudes of good men have been so disgusted with the one-sided, partisan character of the advocates of special ideas and special reforms, that they would have no association with them. We have only to learn that a man can see nothing but his pet idea, and is really in its possession, to lose all confidence in his judgment. When in a court of justice a man testifies upon a point that touches his personal interests or feelings or relations, we say that his testimony is not valuable—not reliable. It decides nothing for us. We say that the evidence does not come from the proper source. We do not expect candor from him, for we perceive that his interests are too deeply involved to allow sound judgment and utterly truthful expression. It is precisely thus with all professional agitators and reformers—all devotees of single ideas. They are personally so intimately connected with their idea—have been so enslaved by their idea—are so interested in its prosperity—that they are not competent to testify with relation to it.

LESSON XVI.

SHYING PEOPLE.

"It is jealousy's peculiar nature
To swell small things to great; nay, out of naught
To conjure much: and then to lose its reason
Amid the hideous phantoms it has formed."

YOUNG.

"I will not shut me from my kind;
And, lest I stiffen into stone,
I will not eat my heart alone,
Nor feed with sighs a passing wind."

TENNYSON.

"Fear is the virtue of slaves; but the heart that loveth is willing."

LONGFELLOW.

READER, did you ever drive a horse that had the mean habit of shying? If so, then you will remember how constantly he was on the lookout for objects that would frighten him. He would never wait for the bugbear to show its head; but he conjured it up at every point. Every hair upon his sides seemed transformed into an eye; and there was not a colored stone, nor a stick of wood, nor a bit of paper, nor a small dog, nor a shadow across the road, nor any thing that introduced variety into his passage, that did not seem to be endowed with some marvellous power of repulsion. First he dodged to the right, after having foreseen the evil from afar, and wrought himself up to a fearful pitch of sidelong excitement; and then he dodged to the left, having been surprised into passing a cat without alarm; and so, dodging to the right and left, he has half worried the life out of you. Being constantly on guard, and always watching for objects of alarm, and suspicious of dangers in disguise, he has had no difficulty in maintaining a condition of permanent fright, which has worked itself off in spasms of shying. To a man who has driven a horse up to a locomotive without danger or fear, such an animal as this seems to be unworthy of the name of a horse; and to one who has read of the spirit and fearlessness of the war-horse, a shying horse seems to be the most contemptible of his race.

Well, I have met shying men, and I meet them upon the sidewalk almost every day. I have watched them from afar, and known by their eyes and a certain preparatory nervousness of body, that they would "shy" at me. I have been conscious, however, that there was nothing in me to shy at. I have had no pistols in my pocket, and no Bowie knife under my coat-collar. I have been innocent of any intention to leap upon and throttle them. I have had no purpose to trip their heels by a sudden "flank movement," and not even the desire to knock their hats off. Indeed, I have felt toward them a degree of friendliness and kindness which I would have been very glad to express, had they afforded me an opportunity; but they were shying men by nature, or by habit, or by whim. So far as I have been able to ascertain the causes of their infirmity, it is the result of a suspicion that they are not quite as good as other people, and a belief that other people understand the fact. Far be it from me to deny that their suspicions touching themselves are well-grounded; but that is no reason why other people should not speak to them politely. There is a class of men and women who are always looking out for, and expecting, slights from those whom they suppose to be their superiors. They get a suspicion that a certain man feels above them; so when they pass him in the street, they shy at him—go around him—will not give him an opportunity to be polite to them. They are martyrs, as they suppose, to unjust social distinctions. They act as if they were painfully uncertain as to whether they are men and women or spaniels.

Now by the side of the person who carries an unsuspicious, self-respectful, open face, into any presence, such people as these seem unworthy of the race to which they belong. It is not the bold, brassy, self-asserting man who is their superior, because his sort of offensive forwardness originates in even a worse state of mind and heart than the habit of shying. When a man shies, he only suspects that he is inferior to his surroundings. When a man offensively puts himself forward, and talks loudly among his betters, he knows he is mean, and knows that he is not where he belongs. You will find a professional gambler to be a loud-mouthed man, who not only does not shy at his betters, but who seeks all convenient opportunities for associating with them, and claiming an equality with them. The shying man is one who has not much respect for himself, who is envious and jealous of others, and who, however strongly he may protest against the charge, has the most abject respect for social position and arbitrary social distinctions. If he see a man who either assumes or seems to be above him, it is a reason in his mind why that man should not notice him. The result is that decent men soon take him at his own valuation, and notice him no more than they would a dog; and they serve him right.

I know of no more thankless task than the attempt to assure shying people that we love them, respect them, and are glad to continue their acquaintance. The instances in which old school-mates meet in the journey of life with a sickening coolness, in consequence of changed circumstances and relations, are of every-day occurrence. Two persons who separated at the school-house door in dawning manhood, with equal prospects, come together later in life. One has risen in the world, has won hosts of friends, has been put forward by them into public office, perhaps, and has acquired a competence. The other has remained upon the old homestead, has had a hard life, and has won neither distinction nor wealth. The fortunate man grasps the hand of the other with all the cordiality of his nature and of his honest friendship; but he meets a reserve which may be almost sullen. He strives to call up the scenes gone by—the old school-sports—the school companions, boys and girls—the old neighborhood friendships—but they will not come. All attempts to touch the heart of his former school-mate, and bring him into sympathy through the power of association, fail. The poor fool suspects his friend of patronizing him, and he will not be patronized. Feeling that his friend has got along in the world better than himself, he cannot understand why he should not be regarded as an inferior, and treated as such. Thenceforward, the fortunate man must seek the society of the unfortunate man, or he will never have it. The former may give practical recognition of entire equality, to the best of his ability, but it will avail nothing, for the latter will not "toady" to his friend, nor be "patronized" by him. At last the fortunate man becomes tired of the effort to make his unfortunate friend understand him, and he kicks him and his memory aside, and calls it a friendship closed forever, without fault upon his part.

I have often wished that it could be understood by these people who are so uncertain in regard to their position, and so suspicious that everybody has the disposition to slight them, and so much afraid of being patronized, and so averse to the thought of "toadying" that they stand stiffly aloof from the society which they envy, and so much offended with people for feeling above them, that their sentiments and feelings are sufficient reasons for society to hold them in contempt. There is a lack of self-respect—a meanness—in their position, that is really a sufficient apology for treating them with entire social neglect. They habitually misconstrue those among whom they move; they are exacting of attention to the last degree; they are always uncomfortable, and they are ready to take offense at the smallest fancied provocation. I have now in my mind an artisan whom I had occasion to get acquainted with a dozen years ago; and I have compelled him to speak to me every time I have met him since. I really do not know what he had done to make him regard himself so contemptuously, but I think he has never to this day fully believed that I have the slightest respect for him. He has tried to dodge me. He has shied repeatedly, but I have compelled him to make me a good-natured bow, till he begins to like it, I think—till he expects it, at least.

Many children are bred to the idea that certain families are socially above them. They are taught from their cradles to consider themselves in a certain sense inferior. How few American children are taught that there is no degradation in poverty, and that a humble employment and an obscure position are entirely consistent with self-respect, under all circumstances, in whatever society. I do not mean to say that they have not heard their parents remark that they were "as good as anybody." There is enough of this talk; and it is precisely this which teaches children that they are born to what their parents consider dishonor,—inferiority to their neighbors. It is impossible for children who have been bred in this way ever to outgrow, entirely, their feeling of inferiority. The people who are entirely self-respectful never have any thing to say about their position in the presence of their children; and it is a cruel thing to teach a child, not that there is a grade of society which is actually above him, but that the persons who occupy that grade look down upon him—and, in the constitution of society, have the right to look down upon him—with contempt. To see an honest lad in humble clothing actually awed by finding himself in the presence of a well-dressed child of affluence, is very pitiful; and there are thousands of these poor boys who, having won wealth and distinction, never in their consciousness lose their early estate sufficiently to feel at home with those among whom the advance of fortune has brought them.

A thoroughly self-respectful person will command respect anywhere. A man who carries into the world an unsuspecting, unassuming face, who is polite to everybody, minds his own business, and does not show by his demeanor that he bears about with him a sense of degradation and inferiority, and who gives evidence that he considers himself a man, and expects the treatment due to a man, will secure politeness and respect from every true gentleman and gentlewoman in the world. The man who shies, and suspects, and envies, and is full of petty jealousies, and is always afraid that he shall not get all that is due to him in the way of polite attention, and manifests a feeling of great uncertainty and anxiety concerning his own social position, is sure to be shunned at last, and he will well deserve his fate. No real gentleman, and no true gentlewoman, ever has feelings like these. It is only those who are neither, and who do not deserve the position of either, that are troubled in this way. I give it as a deliberate judgment that there is far less of contempt for the poor and obscure among what are denominated the higher classes of society than there is of envy and hatred of the rich and renowned among the poor and humble; and that the principal bar to a more cordial and gentle intercourse between the two classes, is the lack of self-respect which pervades the latter, and the mean, degrading humility which they manifest in all their relations with those whom they consider above their level.

American society is mixed—heterogeneous—more so, probably, than that of any other country. There is no such thing as well-defined classification. There is no nobility, no gentry, no aristocracy, no peasantry. The owners of palaces were bred in log cabins; men of learning are the children of boors; and one can never tell by a man's position and relations in society into what style of life he was born. The boy goes into the city from his father's farm, carrying only a hardy frame, a good heart, and a suit of homespun, and twenty years frequently suffice to establish him as a man of fortune, and marry him to a woman of fashion. There is no bar to progress in any direction for the ambitious man, except lack of brains and tact. Society erects no barriers of caste which define the bounds of his liberty. Notwithstanding this, there is always, in every place, a body of people who assume to be "the best society." The claim to the title is rarely well substantiated, and is based on different ideas in different places. We shall find in some places, that society crystallizes around the idea of wealth; in others, around the idea of literary culture; in others, around certain religious views, so that, as it may happen, the "best society" is constituted of the Presbyterian, or Episcopalian, or Unitarian, or other sectarian element. In other places, an old family name is the central power, and, in others still, a certain style of family life attracts sympathetic materials which assume the position of "the best society."

Whatever may be the central idea of the self-constituted elite, they are always the objects of the envy of a large number of minds. Silly people "lie awake nights" to get into the best society. Those who are securely in, of course sleep soundly in their safety and their self-complacency; and those who are too low to think of rising to it, and those who do not care for it, go through the six to ten hours of their slumber "without landing," as the North River boatmen say. But a middle class, who range along the ragged edges of society, know no rest. They sail along in an uncertain way, like the moon on the border of a cloud—sometimes in and sometimes out—feeling naked and very much exposed among the stars, and rather foggy and confused in the cloud, as if, after all, they did not belong there. It is in this class that we meet with shying men and shying women. It is in this class that we find heart-burnings, and jealousies, and envyings, and sensitive misunderstandings. It is a sort of purgatory through which the rising man and woman pass to reach the paradise of their hope, and from which an unhappy soul is never lifted. These people do not stop to inquire whether they have any sympathy, or any thing in common with the society which they seek—whether they would be lost, or whether they would be at home in it. They do not even seem to suspect that much of that which is called the best society, is the last society that a sensible, good man should seek.

Let us suppose that wealth is the central idea of the best society, and then let the aspirant to this society ask himself whether he has wealth. Has he a fine house and an elegant turnout? Does he dress expensively, and is he able to give costly entertainments? Is he prepared to unite, on a plane of perfect equality, with those who give the law to this society? If so, it will not be necessary for him to seek it, for the society will seek him,—that is, if he be an agreeable man. If he be very rich indeed, why, it is not necessary that he be agreeable at all. But suppose literary culture be the central force of this society—has the aspirant any fitness for, or sympathy with it? Can he meet those who form this society as an equal, or mingle in it as a thoroughly sympathetic element? Would he feel happy and at home in a literary atmosphere? These questions indicate a legitimate direction of inquiry, touching every case of this kind. Multitudes of those who are dissatisfied with their position have nothing in common with the society to which they aspire, and would be so much out of place there that they would be very unhappy. My idea, then, is, that so far as society is concerned, men and women naturally find their own place. A true gentleman and a genuine gentlewoman, wherever they may appear, and whoever they may be, are as readily known as any objects; and really good society recognizes its affinities for them at once. They do not have to seek for a place, for they fall into their place as naturally as a soldier falls into, and joins step with, his company.

Now what can be meaner than the jealousy which sits in the circle where it is really most at home, and regards with its green and greedy eyes, a circle for which it has no affinities, except the affinities which envy has for that which it considers above itself? It is a meanness, too, which has two sides to it. It is notorious that the black overseer upon the plantation is severer with his companions in slavery than a white man would be, and it is just as notorious that the man who has abjectly bowed before the distinction of wealth and social standing, always becomes insufferably pretentious when fortune or favor lifts him to the place of his desire. The man who shies those he esteems his betters is always a proud man at heart, or if the adjective be allowable, an aristocratic man; and he is very careful to preserve his position of comparative respectability with relation to those below him. He will always be found to be pretentious in his own circle, and supercilious with relation to those in lower life. Is it not true that half of the neighborhood quarrels that take place, and three-quarters of the slander, and all the gossip that are indulged in, result from these petty jealousies between circles, and the sensitiveness that is felt regarding social standing on the part of those who are not quite so high in the world as they would like to be?

I can only notice briefly the shying that is done by the other side of society. In effect, I have done this already, perhaps, but it is proper to say directly that there are many moving in what is called the best society, who, with a suspicion that they do not belong there, or a feeling that their position is not secure there, shy a humble man when they meet him, and dodge all vulgar associations. I suppose that no true gentleman is ever afraid of being mistaken for any thing else. A gentleman knows that there is nothing which is more unlike the character of a gentleman than the supercilious treatment of the humble, and the fear of losing caste by treating every class with kindness and politeness. I recognize no difference between the two shying classes—the men who shy their fellow-men because they are high, and the men who shy their fellow-men because they are low. Both are mean, both are unmanly, and both are deficient in the self-respect necessary to the constitution of a gentleman. There are no better friends in the world—no men who understand each other better—none who meet and converse more freely at their ease—none who have more respect for each other—than a genuine gentleman and a self-respectful humble man, who knows his place in the social scale, and is abundantly satisfied with it. There is no need of any intercourse between men, of whatever difference of social standing, less dignified and gentle than this.

LESSON XVII.

FAITH IN HUMANITY.

"Say, what is honor? 'Tis the finest sense
Of justice which the human mind can frame,
Intent each lurking frailty to disclaim,
And guard the way of life from all offense,
Suffered or done." WORDSWORTH.

"A child of God had rather ten thousand times suffer for Christ, than that Christ should suffer by Him."—JOHN MASON.

"For mankind are one in spirit, and an instinct bears along
Round the earth's electric circle the swift flash of right or wrong;
Whether conscious or unconscious, yet humanity's vast frame
Through its ocean-sounded fibres feels the gush of joy or shame;—
In the gain or loss of one race, all the rest have equal claim."
LOWELL.

ONE of the most reliable supports of that which is best in man is faith in other men. In truth, I believe that no man can lose his faith in men and women, and remain as good a man as he was before the loss. Better evidence that a man is rotten in some portion of his character, or rotten clean through his character, cannot be found than real, or pretended, loss of faith in his fellows. When a young man tells me that he has no doubt that certain persons, publicly reputed to be good, take sly drinks in their own closets, and descend into grosser indulgences when in strange places; that the best men are hypocrites; that there is no such thing as womanly virtue; and that appetite and selfishness outweigh everywhere principle and manly honor, I know that, ninety-nine times in one hundred, he finds a reason in his own heart and life for his declarations. I know that he simply wishes to maintain a certain degree of self-respect, and that he finds no way to do this save by bringing everybody around him down to his own level. A man who has lost his virtue, and is still suffering under the blows of conscience, is very loth to believe that there is any virtue in the world.

Yet there are circumstances in which faith in humanity is lost without fault, though never without damage, on the part of the loser; and very sad cases they are. I remember an abused, broken-hearted, and forsaken wife, who declared to me her belief that her husband was no worse than other men (pleasant for me, wasn't it?)—that there was not a man in the world who could withstand temptation, or who would have done differently from her husband under the same circumstances. Why was this? She had loved this man with all the devotion of which her warm woman's heart was capable; she had respected him as an embodiment of all manly qualities; he had impersonated her *beau ideal.* If he—the peerless, the prince—could fall, and forsake, and forget, who would not? He who had once been to her the noblest and best man in the world, could never become worse than the rest of the world. Now one of the foulest wrongs and one of the deepest injuries which this man had inflicted upon his wife was the destruction of her faith in men. He had not only blotted out her faith in him, but he had blotted out her faith in humanity, and, of course, her faith in herself. What safeguards of her own virtue fell when her faith in man was destroyed, she did not know; but, in her innermost consciousness, she must have grown careless of herself—possibly desperate.

Hardly a month passes by in which we do not hear of some defalcation, some lapse from integrity, by a man who, through many years of business' life, had maintained an untarnished reputation. I have half a dozen such cases in my memory now, and I do not know what to make of them. When I see a character standing to-day above all reproach, compacted through many years of manly, honest, Christian living, overthrown to-morrow, and trodden in the mire, I am shocked. If such men fall, where are we to look for those who will not? If such men, with worthy natures, and long practice of virtue, and myriad motives for the maintenance of an unspotted character, yield to temptation, and are suddenly overthrown, what reason have I to suppose that my partner, my brother, myself, shall escape? I am scared, and grow cautious, and suspicious.

Did you ever think that there is one individual, at least, in the world—that possibly there are ten individuals, possibly one hundred, possibly more—who believe that you are, as a man or a woman, just as nearly right as you can be? Did you ever think that there are people who pin their faith to you, who believe in you, who trust you, and that among those people your own reputation is identified with the reputation of the race? I care not how humble a man may be, there are always those who trust in him. Think of the trust which a family of children repose in their parents, and of the faith which the parents have in their children. Very humble the parents may be—very untrustworthy as moral guides, and judges, and authorities; but if they were angels, with the light of heaven in their eyes, they would not be more confided in and relied upon by the little ones who cling to their knees. So, at all ages, we garner our faith in individuals; and so, all men and women, however humble and unworthy they may be, become the objects and recipients of this faith.

Now, if there be ten men and women who have garnered their faith in me—who believe in me, through and through—and whose faith in all humanity would be sadly shocked, if I should fall, and prove to them that their confidence had been entirely misplaced, then I hold for those ten persons the reputation of the human race in my hands. If you, my reader, have attracted to yourself the honest faith of a thousand hearts, then you hold in your hands, for those hearts, the good name of humanity. Upon the shoulders of each man in the community, there rests a great responsibility. He has not only his own reputation to take care of, but he has the reputation of his race. If all mankind are to be thought more meanly of by mankind, to be less trusted, and less loved, because I have been untrue, though my untruth touch but one person directly, I commit a great crime against my race. Yet this crime is nothing by the side of that which I commit against those who have trusted in me. It injures them to think meanly of mankind—to have their confidence shaken in humanity—much more than it injures humanity to be thought meanly of. A man may as well stab me as to destroy my faith in my kind, for the comfort and happiness of my life depend upon the maintenance of this faith.

There are not a few men and women in this world who are thoroughly conscious that not only their immediate personal friends think better of them than they deserve, but that the community—all who know them —accord to them a higher excellence of heart and life than they really possess. There are some who seem fitted by nature to attract the affection, and secure the respect of all those with whom they come into contact, in a very remarkable degree; and, yet, these persons may be painfully conscious, all the while, that they are not so good as they are thought to be. They are not hypocrites; they have never intended to deceive anybody; they have never pretended to be what they are not; but people believe in them without limit. A person who has this power of attracting the confidence of men has forced upon him an immense responsibility. To say nothing of his duty to himself and his God, he owes it to his race to be, or to become, as good as he seems. It is essentially a crime against humanity for one who draws the hearts of men to him easily, to do any thing which will tend to depreciate their estimate of his character. A man should carry a life thus extravagantly over-estimated, as he would carry a cup of wine—careful that none be spilled, and careful that no impurity fall into it. It is a great blessing to be loved and respected—nay to be admired for admirable qualities—and when men are generous enough to pay in advance for excellence, they should never be cheated in the amount and quality of the article.

There is such a thing as honor among men; there are such things as modesty, truth, and integrity. They are qualities that belong to humanity, irrespective of religion and of Christian culture. There are men so true to their higher natures that I would trust them with my name, my gold, my children, my all, without a doubt. I am proud to claim kinship with such men. They confer dignity upon the race of which I am a member. I am glad to take their hands in mine. Suppose one of these—for such things have been—should deceive me, and I should discover that my name had been abused, my gold wasted or stolen, and my children ruined by this man: could I ever trust again? Should I not be humiliated? Should I not feel disgraced? Should I ever be willing to let another man into my heart? Should I not doubt whether there are, indeed, such things as honor, and modesty, and truth, and integrity, in the world; and thus doubting, would not the strongest defences of my own virtue be thrown down? The truth is, that no man can do an unmanly thing without inflicting an injury on the whole human race. No man can say "I will do as I choose, and it will be nobody's business." Every man's sin is everybody's business, literally. Every sin shakes men's confidence in men, and becomes, whatever its origin, the enemy of mankind; and all mankind have a right to make common cause in its extermination.

I once heard a careless fellow say that he "professed nothing and lived up to it;" but "professing nothing" does not exonerate a man at all, so far as relates to the personal maintenance of honor, purity, and truth. The man who would excuse a lapse from virtue, or any obliquity of conduct, on the ground that he did not profess any thing, simply announces to me the execrable proposition that every man has a kind or degree of right to be a rascal until he pledges himself to be something better. There are altogether too many men in the world who are keeping themselves easy with the thought that if they are not very good, they never pretended or professed to be,—as if this failure publicly to pronounce themselves on the side of the highest morality, were a sufficient apology for minor delinquencies! It seems to be a poultice of poppies to some sensitively inflamed consciences, that, whatever they may have done, they have never broken promises voluntarily made, to do right—as if there were a release from the obligation to do right, in failing to make the promise! If it will help a man to do right, publicly to profess to do right, and to do good to other men by placing his influence on the right side, then the first duty a man owes to his race, is to make this declaration. But I will not linger here, because my words have led me to the discussion of the obligations of those who have made a profession of Christianity, and taken upon themselves the vows of Christian church-membership.

When a man joins a Christian church, he becomes related to that church in the same way that nature makes him related to humanity. The reputation of the church is placed in his keeping. He cannot do an unchristian thing without injury to the church, or without depreciating, in the eyes of the world, every other member. Think what a blow is inflicted upon the church of Jesus Christ by such scandalous immoralities as some of its most prominent members have been guilty of—by forgeries, and adulteries, and drunkenness! These cases are not common, but when they occur, they are blows under which the church reels. The outside world looks on, and scoffs: "Aha! That's your Christianity, is it?"

I declare that I do not know of a position that more strongly appeals to a man's personal honor than that of membership in a Christian church. Even if a man in such a position should say within himself: "This costs more than it comes to. I love my vices more than I love the Master whose name I profess. Either openly or secretly, I will give rein to my appetites and passions"—he should be arrested by the consideration that he proposes to do that which will wound the feelings, and degrade the position, and injure the influence, of thousands of the best men and women in the world; that he proposes to inflict an irreparable injury upon a cause which has never injured him, and whose office it is to save him, and all mankind. Perhaps he is so weak, and temptation is so strong, that he feels, in the stress of his trial, that he can afford to perjure his own soul; but if he does, he has no right to wound others. Better fight the devil until the animal within us bleeds at every vein—until it dies, if that must be—than "offend one of these little ones." A man who will join a church, and then lead an unchristian life, not only demonstrates before the world his hypocrisy, but he voluntarily undertakes to prove that he has no personal honor. An honorable man will sacrifice himself always before he will voluntarily inflict injury upon a cause he has pledged himself to sustain, and upon men and women whose good name is in his hands. When a member of a church has become so hardened in a course of bad living, that no pang comes to him when he thinks of the injury he is inflicting upon the Christian church, he is bad enough for a prison. I would not trust him the length of my arm.

We have had, within the last ten years, too many notable instances of falls from virtue among the clergy; and every fall has been like an avalanche. They come from a point so near to heaven, and fall so far, that mountain-sides are scarred and whole communities whelmed by the calamity. It takes, often, many years for the villages that lie at their feet to smile again. All Christendom feels the shock, and mourns with downcast eyes the consequences. I freely grant that, as a class, the American clergy, of all denominations, are the purest and best men whom I know; but I cannot resist the conviction that there are many of them who forget what the responsibility is that rests upon them. It was the remark of an aged clergyman, retired from pulpit duties, that if he were a layman he should watch with more anxiety and carefulness than laymen do the relations that exist between pastors and the women of their flock. I do not understand this as a statement that there is any general looseness of conduct among the clergy at all; but as one which covers a kind of impropriety for which there is no name and no punishment. There are women whose affection for their husbands is uprooted through their intercourse with their pastors. There shall never be an improper word spoken; there shall never be a deed committed that would bring a blush to the most sensitive cheek; yet a susceptible woman in the society of a minister of strong and magnetic sympathies, may become as passive as a babe. Led toward him by her religious nature, attracted and held by his intellectual power and the graces of his language, yielding to him her confidence, it is not strange that, before she is aware, she is a captive without a captor, a victim without an enemy, a wreck without a destroyer.

Now I know that there is not a pastor of a strong and graceful and sympathetic nature who reads these words without understanding what I mean—who does not know that there are women in his congregation who are, either consciously or unconsciously, the slaves of his will. I have no doubt that there are some such pastors who will read this essay with a flush of guilt upon their faces. They have never meant these women any ill—they would not harm them for the world—but they are conscious of a selfish and most unchristianly pleasure in these conquests of female natures—these parlor triumphs, God forgive them! Perhaps they go further, and, by the lingering, fervent pressure of a hand, or the glance of an eye, or the utterance of some bit of gallantry or flattery, send into a woman's heart an unwomanly and an unchristian thought. Perhaps they take special delight in the society of some half a dozen female members of their flock, and find themselves dressing for them—betraying to them their weaknesses—opening, in various ways, avenues by which the quick eyes and instincts of these women can see directly into them. The number of pastors is not small, I think, who are not aware that there is one woman, or that there are some women, who know more of what is in them, to their disadvantage, than any man,—that before certain lenient—possibly sad and forgiving eyes—they stand as men who indulge in essentially unchristian vanities of purpose and life.

Of all woman-killers in this world, I know of none so disgusting as one whose chosen profession it is to preach the Gospel of Jesus Christ. A clerical fop, a ministerial gallant, a man who preaches the love of God on Sunday, and lays snares for an innocent heart on Monday afternoon, is a disgrace to Christianity, and a sad burden to the Christian cause. Does such a man think that he can add a little zest to a leisure hour and a humdrum life, by toying with a tender friendship, and giving lease and latitude to his desire for personal conquest, and yet that no one shall know it? Ah, the fallacy! I know of eminent clergymen—earnest workers—who, by yielding to this desire once, have been shorn of their power for good forever, so far as those are concerned who really know them and their weakness. There are ministers in America before whom strong men tremble, and great congregations bow themselves, who could be laughed to scorn and smothered in a cloud of blushes, by some girl to whom, in a weak moment, they betrayed the vain heart that beats within them. Ah! ye men of the black coat and the white neck-cloth,—toying with women, under whatever disguise; indulging in the vanity of personal power, however ingeniously you mask it, is not for you. You can never do it without an injury to the religion which you profess to preach. If you find that you are too weak to resist these temptations—and they are great to such as you—then you should leave the desk forever. You, at least, are bound in personal honor to quit the public advocacy of a cause which your private life dishonors.

Easy to preach, you say? Easier to preach than practise? Nobody knows it better than I—unless it be you. I do not expect perfection in this world, of anybody;—I do not expect impossibilities of anybody. But there are certain duties which men owe to humanity and their race, and which members of Christian churches and teachers of Christian churches owe to Christianity and to their brotherhood, which are possible to be performed, and which I insist upon. I do not appeal to the highest motives—at least I do not appeal to religious motives. I appeal to personal honor. I say that every man, high or low, is bound in honor so to conduct himself as not to disgrace humanity—as not to shake the confidence of men in human honor. I say that every man who belongs to a Christian church—no matter what his internal life may be—is bound in honor so to carry himself before men and women, that the Christian name receive no damage and the Christian cause no prejudice in their eyes. Every man carries the burden of his race and his brotherhood; and if he be a man, he will neither ignore it nor try to shake it off.

LESSON XVIII.

SORE SPOTS AND SENSITIVE SPOTS.

"Canst thou not minister to a mind diseased;
Pluck from the memory a rooted sorrow;
Raze out the written troubles of the brain?"
SHAKSPERE.

"I have gnashed
My teeth in darkness till returning morn,
Then cursed myself till sunset; I have prayed
For madness as a blessing; 'tis denied me."
BYRON.

Alessandra. Methinks thou hast a singular way of showing
Thy happiness!—what ails thee, cousin of mine?
Why didst thou sigh so deeply?

"*Castiglione.* Did I sigh?
I was not conscious of it. It is a fashion,
A silly—a most silly fashion I have
When I am *very* happy. Did I sigh?"
POE.

THERE is a hill opposite to my window, up which, during all the long and weary day, horses are drawing heavy loads. The majority of them crawl patiently along, with their heads down and with reeking flanks and shoulders, pausing occasionally as the water-bars brace the wheels, and impatient only with the flies that vex their ears, and the insufficiency of their short and stumpy tails to protect their quivering sides. Some of these animals are not so patient, but are nervous and spasmodic and unhappy. I have noticed one among them particularly, that has a very bad time every morning with his first load. He is what the teamsters call "balky," though evidently an excellent horse. Much coaxing and not a little whipping seem necessary to get him started; and then he plunges into his work as if he were determined to tear his harness and his load all in pieces. I notice that there are certain unusual fixtures about his collar, and learn that the poor animal has a galled shoulder, so raw and inflamed that all his first efforts in the morning are attended by pain, and that he only works well after the flesh has become benumbed by pressure. I ask his driver why he does not turn the creature into the pasture, and let the ulcer heal, and am told that he has been treated thus repeatedly, but that it always returns when labor is resumed. There is a livery stable that I visit frequently; and while I wait to be served I notice what the grooms are doing. I see that when the curry-comb or brush touches a certain spot upon the horse's skin there is a cringe, and usually a kick and a squeal, —possibly a harmless nip at the groom's shoulder. I learn, too, that there is a certain place upon the back of every horse that the grooms are not permitted to bathe with cold water.

These sore spots and tender spots and sensitive spots on horses have very faithful counterparts in the minds and characters of men. I do not know that I ever met a man who had not on him, somewhere, a sore spot, or a tender spot, or a sensitive spot—a spot that would either gall under the collar of labor, or bring on hysterics if harshly rubbed, or communicate a damaging shock to the nervous system when suddenly cooled. Very few men arrive at thirty-five years of age without getting galled, and very few entirely recover from the abrasion while they live. The spot never thoroughly heals, and the old collar only needs to be put on, even after the longest period of rest, to develop the ulcer in the same old place. I heard a young clergyman preach recently, and I instantly learned that he had a sore spot under his collar. He was a young man of fine powers, bold intellect, a strong love of freedom, and a will determined to do honor to his convictions. He had formed his own opinion upon certain points of doctrine, and had insisted upon it in the presence of his elders. The consequence was that he had been bitterly opposed, and was with great difficulty settled over his parish. The screws had been put tightly down upon him, and he had felt, in the very depths of his sensitive soul, that the liberty wherewith Christ had made him free had been tampered with. So he could neither pray nor preach without showing that he had a sore spot on him. He did not betray it by refusing to draw at all; but he drew violently, as if he had been hitched to the leg of an obtuse Doctor of Divinity, and intended to give all the other Doctors of Divinity notice to get out of the way. Now that sore spot on that young man's shoulder is sure to color all his efforts from this time henceforth, until he puts on another kind of collar. The same old sting will be in all his preaching—a tinge of personal feeling—that the masses of those who hear him preach will not understand, and that he, at last, will become unconscious of. Ministers have more sore places under their harnesses than any class of men I know of.

A minister who has adopted unpopular views, and, in his advocacy of them, has rubbed against the fixed opinions or prejudices of the people to which he is called to preach, is very sure to get sore; and he will either wince with the friction or oppose himself to it with violence. His soreness will always be calling attention to that which caused it, so that if his wound was procured in the advocacy of some infernal doctrine like "infant damnation," why, infant damnation will seem to become a very precious doctrine to him, and he will always be talking about it, and enforcing it. If he has preached against slavery, or intemperance, or any other public wrong or popular vice, and been fiercely and persistently opposed by any portion of his charge, he will betray the sore under his collar on all occasions, and very possibly become so fractious and violent that his flock will be obliged to turn him out to pasture. A minister who gets sore under the friction of any particular collar seems to feel that it is necessary for him to wear that particular collar all the time; and he fails to remember that the reason why he has so much feeling with this collar on, is that it has made him sore. Not unfrequently he becomes so sensitive and so nervous that he kicks out of the traces, and runs away with, and smashes up, the vehicle to which he is attached.

No small degree of the sourness and bitterness and violence of the advocates of special reforms comes from wearing too long the collar of the public apathy, or the public contempt. The men are very few, who, with the consciousness of being actuated by a good motive, can work against opposition a long time, without getting sore, and without betraying their soreness, either by stubbornness or violence. Touch them anywhere but upon the galled spot, and they will be as calm as clocks, and as good-natured as kittens; touch them there, and we are sure to get a kick and a squeal, and a nip at the shoulder. Heartless practical jokers understand where "the raw" is, and know exactly what to say to provoke a galled man to make a fool of himself.

The conscience is very liable to become sore with friction. One entire section of the American nation became sore, even to madness, with working in the collar of the world's condemnation. The slave States of America were very comfortable with slavery so long as they could hold it with self-respect, and so long as the world regarded them rather with sympathy and pity than with condemnation. As the popular opinion against slavery strengthened and became intensified, both in this and other countries, they became sore and sensitive. First, they tucked a constitutional rag between the collar and the skin; and as that did not seem to relieve them, they lined it with leaves from human philosophy; and philosophy soon wearing out, they tore their Bibles into pieces for materials with which to soften the cushion, and set the Christian church to making padding. Every thing failing to produce the desired result, and relieve them of their pain, they refused to draw their portion of the national load, kicked the Union in pieces, and ran away. They will never be happy again until slavery is abolished, or the attitude of the nation and of the world towards slavery is changed. This sore under the collar will never heal, either in or out of the Union, until the cause shall in some way be removed.

It is the same with individuals as with peoples. A man cannot long wear a collar that presses upon his conscience, without getting through the skin—down upon the raw. When a man who sells liquor to his neighbors for drink, voluntarily apologizes to me for it, or justifies himself in it, I know very well that his conscience has a raw place upon it, and that it gives him trouble. When a woman takes particular pains to tell me that she is exceedingly economical, and that she really has had nothing for a year, I cannot but conclude that she has been making some expenditure, or some series of expenditures, that she knows she cannot afford, and that there is a raw place upon her conscience in consequence. In truth, I have never known a woman who wished to impress me with a sense of her rigid economy, who was not more anxious to convince herself of it than me. When a man undertakes to soften the character of any crime by apologies, and by arguments, it is invariably for the purpose of relieving its pressure upon a galled conscience, or shaping it to a different place. I am afraid the men are few who have escaped a galled spot upon their consciences.

Pride has had a terrible time of it in the world. It is, perhaps, the most sensitive spot in human nature. Collars, curry-combs, and cold water have alike served to torment it. A great multitude of men and women have been obliged to work in the collar of poverty, against a galled pride, during all their life. They never start in the morning without flinching, and never work without violence, until their pride has become entirely benumbed by pressure. Ah! if society could be unveiled, how few would be found with pride free from scars and raw places! I once heard a simple boy tell a young man that his legs were crooked; and though the lad was very innocent, and only supposed that he had made and announced a pleasant discovery, he had, alas! hit the man's pride on the very centre of its soreness and sensitiveness. One never knows, in large things, where he will hit the sensitive places in the pride of those he meets; but in little things he is pretty sure to learn it concerning everybody. It is always safe to suppose that a very small man is sore on the subject of bodily dimensions. It will never do for a tall man to propose to measure altitude with him in the presence of women. It is never safe to inquire the age of any lady whom one knows to be more than twenty-five years old. There is not one man or woman in a hundred who possesses an unpleasant personal peculiarity, without getting a galled spot upon personal pride in consequence. A long nose, a squint eye, a clumsy foot, a low forehead, a hump in the back—any one of these will not bear mention in the presence of its possessor.

It is quite amusing to witness the various methods

resorted to for cheating the world with regard to these sore places in personal pride. Men who are conscious that they do not possess a particle of musical taste, and are really ignorant of the difference between Dundee and Yankee Doodle, will profess to be "very fond of music," and will not unfrequently convince themselves that they are so. Men who are exceedingly sensitive touching any eccentricities of person, will be constantly joking about their own long noses, or red hair, or big feet, and run on about them in the pleasantest sort of way, and persist in doing it on all occasions, as if the matter were exceedingly amusing to them, when the fact is that their pride is very sore in that particular spot. A woman who has passed her hour of bloom, and feels with sensitive pain the creeping on of ancient maidenhood, will talk charmingly, and with superfluous iteration, about the usefulness of old maids, and the independence of their lot—determined to cover up the galled spot that burns upon the surface of her personal pride. The trick of keeping up the appearances of wealth, after wealth is departed, is a familiar one; and though it rarely deceives, it is likely to be persisted in to the end of time. It is often very pitiful to witness the ingenuity of the efforts that are made to cover from public observation the soreness of personal pride, caused by a change of circumstances. The Hepsibah Pynchons abound in houses of less than seven gables.

There is probably no harness so apt to gall the shoulder of personal pride as that of ambition. The number of men in the world whose personal pride has a sore on it, inflicted by disappointed ambition, is sadly large. I have seen many a worthy man utterly spoiled by his failure to reach the political, social, or literary eminence at which he has aimed. Thenceforward his hand has been against every man, and he has imagined that every man's hand has been against him. All who contributed to his defeat, and all in any way associated with them, have become the subjects of his hatred and his animadversion. He has retired into himself, sneering at every thing and everybody, doubtful of the sincerity of all friendly professions, and regarding himself as "a passenger," while the poor fools among whom he once so gladly numbered himself, chase the baubles by which his life has been so miserably cheated of its meed. It is very hard for a proud man, with a strong will, to feel that he has been baffled and beaten; and a really noble man, defeated in his objects by trickery and meanness, will sometimes become half insane with the wound which his pride has received. He will never forget it; and the old sore can never be touched, even in the most accidental way, without calling the fire into his eye, and the color into his cheek. In the domain of politics, "sore heads" notoriously abound, and I suppose they always will.

Literary life is probably as prolific of failures, and as full of "sore heads" as political. The number of men and women who are ambitious of literary distinction, and who make great efforts to win it, is very large—larger than the world outside of the publisher's private office dreams of. The number of manuscripts rejected and never published is greater than the number published; and of those which are published, not one in ten satisfies, in its success, the ambition of its author. I suppose that it is within the bounds of truth to say that nine authors in every ten are disappointed men—men whose personal pride is wounded, who believe that the world has treated them unjustly, and who cherish a sore spot on their personal pride as long as they live. Some of these refuse to draw in any harness, and give themselves up to poverty and laziness, as the victims of the world's undiscriminating stupidity. Some become critics of the works of successful authors, and take their revenge in the hearty abuse of their betters. Others enter into other departments of effort, but carry with them through life the belief that they are out of their place, and the conviction that if they had been born in a nobler age they would have been recognized as the geniuses they imagine themselves to be.

There is still another class which get sore with drawing in a harness that God puts upon them, and in the adoption of which they have had nothing to do.

A man of poetic sensibilities finds himself engaged in the pursuit of some humdrum calling. He sees how beautiful poetry is; he feels its influence upon his soul; but he has no power to create it. Another feels something of the divinity of music, but muscular facility has been denied to him so that he cannot play, and his voice is harsh or feeble so that he cannot sing. He melts and glows under the sway of eloquence, and worships at a distance the power of the orator over the hearts and minds of men; but he knows that if he were in the orator's place, he would break down and become the object even of his own contempt. Great susceptibilities these people have—passive spirits—open to all good impressions, appreciative of that which is best in nature and art, yet without the power to act. They must always be plates to receive the picture, and never suns and cameras to imprint it. They must always live within sight of great and beautiful powers, but never have the privilege of wielding them. Doomed to the attitude of receptivity, they see that they can never change it; and that they can never be to others what others are to them. Thus they grow sore with the thought of their weakness, and a sense of the circumscription of their faculties. They see wonderful things —they apprehend the grace and the glory of great actions—but they can achieve nothing. Many of these walk as in a dream through life—with a sense of wings upon their shoulders, clipped or lashed down. They see their companions rising, but they cling to the earth, and feel the difference as a humiliation. Alas! how many souls chafe against the consciousness of inferior powers, till even the fine susceptibilities with which nature endowed them are destroyed!

There would seem to be no end of the causes which produce sore and tender and sensitive spots upon the human soul. I have said nothing of grief and love and pity and anger, and a whole brood of powerful passions, but they are all operative toward the results which we are discussing. The cure for these sensitive sores is obvious enough. I would prescribe for a man as I would for a horse—go out to pasture, or adopt another kind of collar, and never wear the old one again. If a man has become sore by working against the apathy, the misconceptions, the misconstructions, and the prejudices of the world, so that he feels the galling burden of the collar in all his actions, let him change his style of labor until the ulcer heal. If the conscience becomes sore, relieve it of that which made it sore, and never believe that padding can effect a cure. Even wounded pride will heal if we let it alone, and refrain from opening the wound on all occasions, and rubbing it against the causes which inflicted it. All the natural peculiarities of our constitution which wound our pride may be happily got along with by ignoring them. If my neighbor is a lovable man, I do not love him any the less because he wears a long nose, and I should never think of it if he were not always joking about it, and trying to convince me that it did not offend him. A man who quarrels with his own constitution, and questions the benevolence that adjusted it to its conditions, quarrels with, and questions, his Maker. I believe there are no sorenesses of the sort we are considering which time or change will not heal.

It seems to me a very melancholy thing for a man to carry a mental ulcer with him through life—to feel its prick and pang in every effort—to be conscious of its presence every hour—to be engaged in covering it from sight, or in the attempt to deceive the world with regard to it. Life is altogether too good a thing to be spoiled by a little sore, or a large one, when there exists an obvious mode of cure. It is our immense and intense self-consciousness that stands in our way always in this matter. The truth is that the world does not think half so much about us as we imagine it does. A man may walk through the city of New York with a face "as homely as a hedge-fence," thinking about it all the time, and wondering what people think of it, and not a man of all the throng will even see it. It is so in the world at large. Our personal peculiarities, our personal failures, our personal weaknesses, our personal affairs generally possess very little interest for others. They have enough to do in taking care of themselves, and have weaknesses, and failures, and peculiarities enough of their own; and if the world should spurn our well-meant efforts in its behalf, why, let it go. It mends nothing to get sore and sensitive over it. When a man truly learns how little important he is in the world, he is generally beyond the danger of becoming galled by his harness, whatever it may be.

LESSON XIX.

THE INFLUENCE OF PRAISE.

"Now I praise you, brethren, that ye remember me in all things, and keep the ordinances as I delivered them unto you."—St. Paul.

"O popular applause! What heart of man
Is proof against thy sweet seducing charms?"
Cowper.

"*Arbaces.* Why now, you flatter.
"*Mardonius.* I never understood the word."
A King and no King.

"Praising what is lost
Makes the remembrance dear."
Shakspere.

IT is pleasant to be praised. The man does not live who is insensible to honest praise. The love of approbation is as natural to every human soul as the love of offspring, or the love of liberty. It was planted there by God's hand, and it is as useful and important in its fruit, as it is fragrant and beautiful in its flower. I repeat that the man does not live who is insensible to honest praise. That great orator who seems to be a king in the world, independent of his race, holding dominion over human hearts, lifted far above the necessity of the plaudits of those around him, will pause with gratified and grateful ear, to listen to expressions of approval and admiration from the humblest lips. The greatest mind drinks praise as a pleasant draught, if it be honest and deserved. Perhaps you think that Doctor of Divinity who weighs two hundred pounds more or less, and is clad in glossy broad-cloth, and lifts his shining forehead above a white cravat, as Mont Blanc pierces a belt of cloud, and talks articulated thunder, and veils his wisdom behind gold-mounted spectacles, and moves among men with ineffable dignity, is above the need of, and the appetite for, praise. Ah! you don't know the soft old heart under that satin waistcoat! It can be made as warm and gentle and grateful, with just and generous praise, as that of a boy. Nay, the barber who takes his reverent nose between his thumb and finger, and sweeps the beard from his benevolent chin, understands exactly what to say in order to draw from his pocket an extra sixpence. There is no head so high, there is no neck so stiff, there is no back so straight, that it will not bend to take the flowers which praise tosses upon its path.

"It's a sign of weakness, after all," sighs my friend, who is not praised quite as much as he would like to be. Begging your pardon, sir, it is no such thing.

The strongest Being in the universe—the God of the universe—is the one who demands, receives, and accepts the most praise. Listen for a moment to those marvellous ascriptions which rise to Him from the bosom of Christendom as ceaselessly and beautifully as clouds from the Heaven-reflecting ocean: "Thou art the King, immortal, invisible. Thou art the Source of all life, the Author of all being, the Fountain of all light and love and joy. Thou art Love itself; Thou art the Sum of all perfections. For what Thou art, we worship Thee; for what Thou hast done for us, in Thy infinite loving-kindness, we praise Thee. We bless Thy Holy Name. We call upon our souls and all within us to magnify Thy name forever and ever." The Bible itself has given us almost numberless forms of expression into which we may cast our divinest adoration, and the broadest outpourings of our hearts. The poets of all ages have been touched to their finest utterances in the rapture of worship and of praise.

Now why should God want praise of us? It certainly is not because He is weak. Can it be because He wishes by means of it to produce some desired effect in us? Is there no hearing of this praise in Heaven? Are we who sing and shout mere brawlers, who get a little strength of lungs by the exercise? There are some poor souls, doubtless, who believe this, as they believe that prayer has significance only as a moral exercise, and effect only as it reacts upon the soul. I believe that praise is pleasant to Him who sits upon the throne—that the honest and sincere expressions of love and adoration, and gratitude and praise, that rise to Him from the earth are at least shining ripples upon the soundless ocean of His bliss. Out from Him proceed, through myriad channels of effluence, the expressions of His love for those whom He has made and endowed with intelligence; and I believe that it is requisite for His happiness that back along these lines of manifestation there should flow a tide of grateful recognition and adoring praise. Even a God would pine in loneliness and despair if there should come back no echoes to His loving voice—no refluent wave to the mighty bosom which makes all shores vocal with its breath and beating. God demands of all men that which all men owe to Him—that which His perfections and His acts deserve.

This love of approbation in men, then, is Heavenborn and Godlike. The desire for approbation is as legitimate as the desire for food. I do not suppose that it should be greatly a motive of action—perhaps it should never be; but when a man from a good motive does a good thing, he desires the approval of the hearts that love him, and he receives their expressions of praise with grateful pleasure. Nay, if these expressions of praise are denied to him, he feels in a certain sense wronged. He feels that justice has not been done him—that there is something due to him that has not been paid. I met a friend the other day who unveiled his heart to me; and I caught in the vision his heart's sense of the world's injustice. He had been a very poor boy, and had been bred under a poor boy's disadvantages; but a strong will, a good heart, fine talents, and a favoring fortune, brought to him gold, and lands, and equipage. They brought these not only, but they brought the power to be a benefactor of his native town. He won competence for himself, and then he became a public-spirited citizen, and did that for his home which no other man had done. Now he felt that he had done for himself and for those around him nobly; and it was natural that he should desire some response—some expression of praise. He did not get it. People either envied him, or they misconstrued his actions; and he felt that his townsmen had been and were unjust—that they owed him something which they had failed to pay.

The world is so much accustomed to confound praise with flattery that if I were to go to a man with an honest tribute like this: "My friend, I admire you very much; I think you possess noble talents, fine tastes, and an excellent heart; and I regard your course of action and your life with the warmest approval," he would, nine times in ten, look into my face either with astonishment, or amusement, or offense. He would not know whether I intended to insult him or to practice a joke upon him. Praise between man and man is so rare that we neither know how to bestow it nor how to receive it. This is carried to such an extent that one-half of the family life of Christendom is deprived of it. The husbands who never have a word of praise for their wives, the wives who never have a word of praise for their husbands, and the parents who only find fault with their children, are, I fear, in the majority. I know that the women are numberless who devote themselves throughout all their life to the comfort, the happiness, and the prosperity of their husbands, and who lie down in their graves at last, thirsty for their praise. Their patient and ceaseless ministry is taken as a matter of course, without the slightest recognition of its value as the expression of a loving and devoted heart. Now I believe that praise is due to the love and unselfish devotion of a wife, just as really as it is to the loving-kindness and beneficent ministry of God, differing only in kind and degree. Husbands may die worth millions, and leave it all to their wives, (subject to the usual contemptible provision that they do not marry again,) and yet be shamefully indebted to them forever and forever.

Children are often spoiled because they get no credit for what they do. Of censure, they get their due; but of praise, never. They do a thing which they feel to be praiseworthy, but it is not noticed. When a child takes pains to do well, it feels itself paid for every endeavor by praise; and the most unsophisticated child knows when praise is its due. It often comes to its mother's knee in natural simplicity, and asks for it. It is very well for men to say that "virtue is its own reward," and that the highest satisfactions are those which spring from a sense of duty accomplished; but praise is pleasant and precious to men who not only say this, but feel it. Many a noble and sensitive pastor is disheartened because no one of the multitude which he so carefully and constantly feeds, ever tells him, with an open, honest utterance, his good opinion of him, and his satisfaction with his labors. Many an excellent author toils over his work in secret distrust, and issues it in fear and trembling, feeling that a word of praise will exalt him into a grateful and fruitful joy, and that an unjust and unkind criticism will half kill him.

It is true that the mind is unhealthy which lives on praise; and it is just as true that he is mean and unjust who fails to award praise to those who earn it. The appetite for praise may become just as morbid and greedy by improper stimulus and abuse, as any other natural and legitimate appetite. It frequently does so, in those who associate it very intimately with success and gain. Actors and public singers, and all those whose success in life and whose pecuniary income depend upon the amount of popular praise they can win, are very apt to become greedy of praise, and will not unfrequently receive it in its most disgusting forms. There are lecturers and public speakers who depend upon praise for strength to speak an hour—men who, if their performances are repetitions, wait at certain points for applause, as a horse, travelling over a familiar road, stops always at certain hills to rest and take breath, and at certain wayside cisterns to drink. Many of these men demand praise, talking about themselves continually, and begging assent to their self-laudations. In these cases, praise becomes the dominant motive, and degrades and belittles its subjects always. The voluntary profanity and the impure jests that so often offend the ears of decent people at the theatre, are put forth to call out a cheer from groundlings whose praise is always essential disgrace. The jealousy and the quarrelsomeness of authors, actors, and singers, result from the fact that praise has become so much the motive of their life that they grudge the applause awarded to their fellows.

The difference between praise and flattery is as wide as that between praise and blame. Praise is a legitimate tribute to worth and worthy doing. It is entirely unselfish in its motive. It is the discharge of a debt. Flattery originates always in a selfish motive, and seeks by falsehood to feed an unhealthy desire for praise. A man whom it is proper to praise cannot be flattered, and a man who can be flattered ought not to be praised. It is always safe to praise a man who really deserves praise. Such a man usually knows how much he deserves, and will take only the exact amount. Indeed, he will be very particular to give back the right change. The flatterer is like the man who stands behind a bar to deal out poison to a debased appetite for gain. The man who utters honest praise is noble; the man who receives it does so without humiliation, and is made strong by it. The flatterer is always a scoundrel, and the glad receiver of his falsehoods is always a fool—natural or otherwise.

The desire for praise is often very strong in those who never do any thing to deserve it, and who are never ready to award it to those who have earned it. There are men in every community who are universally recognized as supremely selfish, yet supremely greedy of praise. This desire does not arise from over-indulgence in the article, for they never had even a taste of it. They are known to be selfish and hard and mean, yet they long for praise and popularity, with a desire that is almost ludicrous. They never give a dollar to the poor, they never deny themselves for the good of others, they are shut up in themselves —without any good or great or generous qualities—

yet they clutch at every word that sounds like praise as if they were starved. The only use of the desire in these men is to furnish the world with a nose by which to lead them.

It is a mistake to suppose that praise should be rendered directly in all cases to the persons to whom it is due, for the relations between debtor and creditor may be such as to forbid it. I may be a humble admirer of some great and good man, who has been the doer of great and good deeds, but my personal relations to him may be such that it is not proper for me to approach him, and pay my tribute into his hands. Men are often careful of the channels through which the response to their deeds, in the hearts of other men, reaches them; but I may discharge my debt, nevertheless, by sounding their praise in other ears. It is usually the work of those who stand next to a man, to gather up the tributes of a grateful and admiring community or people, and bear them to him to whom they belong. Because I may not approach a praiseworthy man, with the offering which I feel to be his due, it is none the less incumbent upon me to discharge the debt. Just and generous praise will come from every just and generous nature in some form, and will be deposited in some bosom subject to the draft of the owner.

It is not easy for any man to work alone, out of the sight of his fellows, and beyond the recognition of his deeds. However self-sufficient he may be, he is stronger, and he feels stronger, in the approbation of generous and appreciative hearts. We are very much in the habit of thinking that men of great minds and noble deeds and self-reliant natures do not need the approval of other minds, and do not care for it; but God never lifted any man so far above his fellows that their voices were not the most delightful sounds that reached him. If this be true of great natures, how much more evidently true is it of smaller natures! We, the people of the world, go leaning on each other; and we totter sometimes, even to falling, when a shoulder drops from underneath our hand. We need encouragement with every step. In the path of worthy doing, we need some loving voice to witness with our approving consciences, that we have done that which becomes us as men and women. We long to hear the sentence, "well done, thou good and faithful servant," from day to day; and when we hear it, we are ready for further labor. We need also to give this daily meed of praise to those who deserve it, that we may keep ourselves unselfish, and root out from ourselves all niggardliness. We owe it to ourselves to pay off every debt as soon as it is incurred, and never, under any selfish motive, to withhold it.

It is notorious that the finest spirits of the world, and the world's greatest benefactors, have gone through life unrecognized. They have lain down in their graves at last without having received a tithe of the debt which their generation owed to them. When the turf has closed over their bosoms, and the mean jealousies of their cotemporaries have been vanquished by death, then whole nations have thronged to do them honor. Songs have been sung to their memory; and the words of praise which would have done so much to cheer and strengthen them once, are poured out in abundance when the need of them is past. Stately monuments are erected to them, and their children are petted and caressed, and a tardy, jealous, and hypocritical world strives to win self-respect by the payment of a debt long overdue. "Speak nothing but good of the dead" is a proverb that had its birth in the world's sense of its own meanness,—the consciousness that it had not done justice to the dead while they were living. Many a man is systematically abused during all his active life, only to lie down in his grave amid the laudations of a nation. I know of nothing in all the exhibitions of human nature meaner than this. It amounts to a virtual confession of fraud. It is the acknowledgment of a debt, which, while the creditor could get any benefit from it, the world refused to pay. Posthumous fame may be a very fine thing; but I have never known a really worthy man, with a healthy nature and a healthy character, who did not prize far above it the love, the confidence, and the praise of the generation to which he gave his life.

It is the mark of a noble nature to be quick to recognize that which is praiseworthy in others, and ready on the moment to award to it its fitting meed. Such a nature looks for that which is good in men, sees it, encourages it, and gives it the strength of its indorsal. All that is noble in other men thrives in the presence of such a nature as this. It is sunshine and showers and healthful breezes to all that is amiable and laudable in the souls around it. Woman grows more womanly and lovable and happy in its presence. Men grow heroic and unselfish by its side. Children gather from it encouragement and inspiration, and impulse and direction into a beautiful life. What knows the charming wife whom we lay in the tomb, of the tears we shed above her, of the endearments we lavish upon her memory, and of the praises of her virtue with which we burden the ears of our friends? This same wife would have drunk such expressions during her life with satisfaction and gratification beyond expression. Why can death alone teach us that those whom we love are dear? Why must they be placed forever beyond our sight before our lips can be unsealed? Why must it be that in our public, social, and family life we have penalties in abundance, but no rewards—censure in profusion, but no praise—fault-finding without stint of freedom, but approbation dealt out by constrained and niggardly hands?

LESSON XX.

UNNECESSARY BURDENS.

"I groan beneath this cowardice of heart
Which rolls the evil to be borne to-day
Upon to-morrow, loading it with gloom."
ALEXANDER SMITH.

"There are two ways of escaping from suffering; the one by rising above the causes of conflict, the other by sinking below them; for there is quiet in the soul when all its faculties are harmonized about any centre. The one is the religious method; the other is the vulgar, worldly method. The one is called Christian elevation; the other, stoicism."—BEECHER.

THERE were few houses of the old time in New England that did not contain a well-thumbed volume of the Pilgrim's Progress; and there were few children who did not become acquainted with its contents, either through its text or its pictures. I am sure that all the children felt as I did—very tired with sympathy for the poor pilgrim who was obliged to lug that ugly pack from picture to picture, and very "glad and lightsome" when at last it fell from his shoulders, and went tumbling down the hill. We did not marvel that "he stood still awhile, to look and wonder," or that "he looked, and looked again, even till the springs that were in his head sent the waters down his cheeks." It was a great thing for a man who was bent on progress to be freed from an unnecessary burden; and it may be pleasant to know that at the foot of the hill of life the same sepulchre which swallowed the burden of Bunyan's Pilgrim, so that he "saw it no more," still stands open, and has room in it for all the burdens of all the pilgrims there are in the world.

I wonder whether all the pilgrims who have undertaken the journey "from this world to that which is to come" ever lose the pack whose fastenings were so quickly dissolved when our favorite old Pilgrim looked upon the Cross? I doubt it. I hear many people groaning throughout the whole course of their Christian experience with the oppressive weight of this same burden. Instead of losing it at the sight of the cross, they hold to it, and will not let it go. They mean well enough; but they do not understand that the cross was reared, and the meek sufferer nailed to it, that the burden of the penitent soul might be forever rolled off. They carry their own sins, and never yield the pack to Him who bore it for them "in His own body, on the tree." They are never "light and gladsome" with a sense of great relief; and their Christian progress is sadly impeded by the burden from which the central truth of the Christian scheme releases them. If there be any such thing as forgiveness, then there is such a thing as release; but I think there are many subjects of free and full forgiveness who insist on carrying their old, dirty packs to their graves, staggering under them all the way.

But this is not what I started to write about. A great many men carry their life as an author carries a book which he is writing—never losing the sense of their burden. When a writer undertakes a book, and feels the necessity of perfect continuity of thought and symmetry of structure, he can never lay it wholly aside. When once he has taken up the first chapter, and comprehended his materials and machinery and end, he does not dare to lay down his work, or diverge from the grand channel of his thought, until the last chapter is finished. He can take no three months' vacation; he can read no books that do not contribute to his progress in the chosen direction; he can never wholly lay aside the burden that is on him. It is like lifting upon one's shoulder the end of a long pole, and then walking under it from end to end. The burden upon the shoulder is not relieved until the whole length has been passed, and it drops as we walk from under it. Such is the way that many men, and, perhaps, most men, carry life. If their business troubles them, they have no power to throw it off, and no disposition to try to do it. They are entirely aware that they gain nothing by carrying their tedious burden, but they carry it. Not content with doing their duty, and trying their best while actively engaged, they take home with them a long face, breathe sighs around them in the saddest fashion, and really unfit themselves for the healthy exercise of their reason, and the active employment of their faculties.

With men of this stamp, it makes little difference whether they are prosperous or otherwise. If times are good, and they really have no fault to find with matters as they exist, they become troubled about bad times that may possibly lie just ahead. "Oh, it's all well enough to-day," they say, "but you can't tell what is coming;" so they bind the burden of the future upon them, and undertake to steal a march on God's providence. Such a thing as doing the duty of a single day, and doing it well, and then throwing off the burden of care, and having a good time in some rational way, until the hour comes for the commencement of the next day's duty, they are strangers to. They walk into their houses with a cloud upon their faces. They have no words of cheer for those whom they have left at home during the day. They are moody and sullen and sad—absorbed by their troubled thoughts—taking no interest in the schemes, and having no sympathy with the trials, of their wives and children, and making no effort to relieve themselves of their burdens. If they pray at all, they practically pray like this: "Give us this day our daily bread, and to-morrow, and next day, and the day after, and next year, and fifty years to come; and lest Thou shouldst forget it, or neglect to answer us, we have undertaken to look after the matter ourselves."

To say nothing of the constant sadness, uneasiness, and discomfort of such a life as this, to all those who lead it, and to all who are intimately associated with them, the permanent effect of it upon the character of its subjects is to make them selfish and hard, and small and mean. Whatever may be their circumstances, they become sensitive upon any expenditure of money for purposes beyond the simplest necessities of personal and family life. This result is both natural and inevitable. A man whose life, in and out of his counting-room, is absorbed by business, ceases, at last, to be any thing but a man of business; and his mind contracts and hardens down to its central, motive idea. That which becomes the dominant aim and the grand end of life, always determines the character of life; and I have known young men, even before they have approached middle age, to become mean and miserly to such a degree as to disappoint and disgust their friends, simply in consequence of a few years' absorption in business. Business is not life, nor is it life's end.

It is simply a means of life; and all true living lies outside of it. Ministry is the mission of business—ministry to necessity, to comfort, and to a personal, family, and social life into which business never enters, save with an unwelcome foot and a disturbing hand. This everlasting hugging of the burden of business, is, therefore, not only a painful task, but it is permanently damaging to all who indulge in it.

"It is very easy to talk," says my friend, with a load upon his shoulders, "but talking does not pay notes at the bank, and keep creditors easy, and provide for one's family." Granted: and now will you be kind enough to tell me how many notes you ever paid at bank, and how much provision you ever made for your family by "mugging" over your troubles out of business hours? If your retort is good for any thing, mine is. You never accomplished one good thing in your life by making yourself and others unhappy through constant dwelling upon trouble when not engaged in active efforts to extricate yourself from it. You never gained a single inch of progress by dwelling upon miscarriages in business which you could not avoid. All your absorption, all your sad reflection, all your misgivings about the future, all your care beyond the exercise of your best ability in action, has not only been utterly useless, but it has injured the comfort of all around you, destroyed the peace of your life, cheated you out of the reward of your labor, and made a smaller, harder, meaner man of you. If any good result could be secured by carrying the burden of your business into all your life, then there would be some apology for it; but you know that no such result can be secured. "It is very easy to talk," my friend persists in saying, "but one cannot always command one's mind, in such a matter as this." Did you ever try? Have you ever systematically tried to do this? Is it your regular aim, after you have discharged the business of the day, to throw off care until the next day's business is undertaken? No? Then how do you know whether it is easy or not?

I believe it is in the power of every man, who has not too long abused himself, to lay aside every night his pack of mental care and anxiety, and enter into life. Not only this, but I believe that it is absolutely essential to his business success that he do this. A man who dwells constantly upon the dark side of his affairs, and is troubled and gloomy in his apprehensions concerning the future, becomes a weak and timid man—disqualified in many essential respects for the work of his life. His mind needs rest and revivification. Suppose an ass were to be treated in the manner in which men treat themselves. Suppose the burden which we place upon him during the day were kept lashed to his back at night, so that he must bear it, either standing or lying, off duty as well as on. How long would he be worth any thing for labor? The illustration is apposite in every particular. If the mind is to be kept fit for business, it is at regular periods to be kept out of business. A great multitude of business failures are attributable, I have no doubt, to the debilitating and damaging effect of carrying the burdens of business between business hours. Men become in a measure sick and insane by dwelling upon their affairs, when they should be receiving rest and refreshment.

Again, men who insist upon keeping their packs upon their shoulders, practically deny the existence of the providence of a Being superior to themselves, and dominant in all human affairs. If I were to say to one of these men: "you do not believe in Providence at all," he would accuse me of a harsh judgment, and feel injured by it; but it is certainly legitimate for me to ask him what evidence he gives of his belief. All, indeed, profess to believe in Providence, in a certain general way. The popular idea is very foggy upon the matter. We somehow imagine that God knows every thing in general and nothing in particular—that He takes interest in, supervision of, and controlling influence over, matters at large, with an imperial disregard of details—that He moulds with a majestic hand the character and destiny of nations, but never condescends to meddle with the small and insignificant affairs of individuals. Providence, in this view, would seem to be very much like certain tongs used in a blacksmith's shop, whose jaws do not wholly close—convenient for handling large pieces of iron, but incapable of grasping a nail. Or, Providence is like a great general, who only directs the movements of large bodies of men, deals only with the officers, and never thinks of so small a thing as looking after the blanket of a private soldier, or dressing a wounded finger.

It is very easy to perceive that such a Providence as this has no practical value in every-day, individual life. Very evidently it is not that Providence which numbers the hairs of men's heads, and without whose notice not a sparrow falls to the ground. One is a Providence made by men who undertake to measure God by themselves; the other is the Providence revealed in the Bible. God exercises a special providence, which reaches to the minutest affairs of the most insignificant man, or we are all in a condition of essential orphanage. A special Providence denied, and prayer becomes a mockery, devotion a deceit, and the sense of individual responsibility slavery to a superstitious idea. Now I do not pretend to address myself to men who do not believe in prayer. I know men well enough to know that there are very few of them who do not believe in prayer, and that there are very few of them who do not, particularly in moments of danger, pray.

Deep down under the thickest crusts of depravity there lies the conviction, always ready to rise in painful emergencies, that God takes cognizance of every man, and is able to help him. Smooth away the idea of Providence as we may, into an unmeaning generality, the time comes, in every man's life, when he recognizes the fact that God is dealing with him; and he may as well recognize the fact all the time as when he is driven to feel that he has no help in himself.

So, if there be a special Providence, it is a Providence to be trusted; and the man who believes in it has no apology for carrying a single unnecessary burden. This providence in all human affairs, is like the principle of vitality in the vegetable world. It does not release us from effort, in every legitimate and needful way, for the accomplishment of our laudable purposes; but when our efforts are complete, it takes care of the rest. What should we think of the farmer who could never roll the burden of his cornfield from his mind, and who, after hoeing his ground repeatedly, and cutting or covering every weed, should go night after night and sit up with it, and think of it, and dream of it all the while? He has done all there is for him to do, and beyond this he cannot control an hour of sunshine, a drop of dew, or a single cloud-full of rain. He cannot influence the law of growth in any particular. His field is in the control of a power entirely above and beyond him; and every thought he gives to it, after having done what he can for its prosperity, is utterly useless. It is his business to trust. Having done what he can, the remainder is in the hands of Him who feeds the springs of being with light and heat and moisture. It is thus that man's affairs grow while he sleeps. The hand that ministers to every plant will not fail to minister to him for whose use the plant was made.

Why do not men trust in Providence? Simply because, in their usual moods and in their usual circumstances, they do not believe in it. There is no other explanation. You, my friend, who carry your burdens around on your shoulders all the time, and who, perhaps, pray every morning and every night, do not believe in Providence. You do not feel that you can trust Providence. You assent to all that I say upon the subject, but, after all, your belief in Providence has no genuine vitality. You do not believe in it as you believe in the purity of your wife or the honor of your friend. You do not rely upon it for an hour. You do nod your head and say—"yes, yes;" and you think you are sincere; but you deceive yourself. So long as you persist in carrying your pack, which is a very unpleasant burden, as you know, you do not believe in Providence; else you would trust in it. You are tired and harassed by your daily labor; and it is very natural to suppose that if you could remove your burden each evening, and place it in the charge of one whom you believe would take care of it, you would do it with gladness. You fail to do it, and what is the natural conclusion? It is that your belief in Providence is a humbug. You believe in the honor of your friend, and you trust it. You believe in the honesty and ability of your creditor, and you trust him. You trust every thing and everybody that you firmly believe in; and the only reason under heaven why you do not roll off the burden that oppresses you, every day and every hour of your life, and commit it to the care of Providence, is, that you do not believe in Providence.

We are in the habit of talking about the world as a world of care, and speaking of human life as inseparably accompanied by trouble. This is, indeed, the truth; but if we were to remove from the world all its useless care, and take from life all its unnecessary trouble, they would be transformed into such bright and pleasant things that we should hardly know them. I know very few men and women who do not bear about with them care and trouble which God never put upon them, and which He has no desire to see upon their shoulders. It does not belong to them. It relates to things that are in the realm of Providence alone, or to things over which they have no control. The future is God's, but they voluntarily take it upon their shoulders, and try to bear it. They pluck a section of God's eternity out of His hands, and groan with the burden. They assume care which is not their own—which belongs to the Controller of their lives, and the Governor of the universe. It is care for that which is beyond human care—anxiety for that which anxiety cannot reach—trouble about that which we can neither make nor mend—that oppresses humanity. We can bear our daily burdens very well. We can go through our regular hours of bodily and mental labor, and feel the better rather than the worse for it; but to care for that which our care cannot touch, and to be troubled about that which is entirely beyond our sphere—this is the burden that breaks the back of the world—this is the burden which we bind to our shoulders with obstinate fatuity.

LESSON XXI.

PROPER PEOPLE AND PERFECT PEOPLE.

"I must have liberty
Withal, as large a charter as the wind
To blow on whom I please."
SHAKSPERE.

"They say best men are moulded out of faults."
THE SAME.

"There's no such thing in nature, and you'll draw
A faultless monster which the world ne'er saw."
SHEFFIELD.

NATURE calls for room and for freedom—room for her ocean and freedom for its waves; room for her rivers and freedom for their flowing; room for her forests and freedom for every tree to respond to the influences of earth and sky according to its law. Exceedingly proper things are not at all in the line of nature. Nature never trims a hedge, or cuts off the tail of a horse. Nature never compels a brook to flow in a right line, but permits it to make just as many turns in a meadow as it pleases. Nature is very careless about the form of her clouds, and masses and colors them with great disregard of the opinions of the painters. Nature never thinks of smoothing off her rocks, and cleaning away her mud, and keeping herself trim and neat. She does very improper things in a very impulsive manner. Instead of contriving some safe, silent, and secret way to dispose of her electricity, she comes out with a blinding flash and a stunning crash, and a rush of rain that very likely fills the mountain streams to overflowing, and destroys bridges and booms, and cabins and cornfields. On the whole, though nature keeps up a respectable appearance, I suppose that, in the opinion of my particular friend Miss Nancy, she would be improved by taking a few lessons of a French gardener, and reading savage criticisms on Ruskin.

I have alluded to my particular friend Miss Nancy. Perhaps I ought to say, at starting, that Miss Nancy is a man, and that I use the name bestowed upon him by his enemies, because it is, in a very important sense, descriptive. Miss Nancy's boots are faithfully polished twice a day. His linen is immaculate; and the tie of his cravat is square and faultless. He never makes a mistake in grammar while engaged in conversation. He is versed in all the forms and usages of society, and particularly at home in gallant attention to what he calls "the ladies." He seems to have lost every rough corner, if he ever had one. In politics and religion, he is just as proper as in social life. The most respectable religion is his religion; and the politics that shun extremes are his politics. I think he is what they call a conservative. At any rate, I never knew him to do a rash or impulsive thing, or speak an improper word in his life. I think he is as nearly perfect as any man I ever saw.

But, after all, Miss Nancy is not a popular man. He will probably live and die an old bachelor, because all the women will persist in laughing at him. He is certainly good-looking, his dress is unexceptionable, his manners are "as good as they make them," and his morals are as proper as his manners; yet I have not yet seen the woman who would speak a pleasant word of my friend. He is decidedly a "woman's man," yet no woman will own him, and no woman feels comfortable with him. His language is so carefully guarded against all impropriety of style and structure, that she feels as if he were criticizing every word she utters, as well as measuring his own. His manners are so very proper that they are formal and constrained, and make her uncomfortable. His sentiments and opinions are so very conservative, that they have no vitality in them. With a curious perverseness, the most gentle and accomplished women will turn from him with a sense of relief, to join in the society of a hearty fellow with a loud laugh and a dash of slang, and a free and easy way with him. It may be difficult to explain all this, but it is true. An exceedingly proper man is never a popular man. That life which is controlled by rigid and unvarying rules, and regulated by conventionalities in every minute particular, and restrained in every impulse by notions of propriety, is unlovely and unnatural, and can never be otherwise.

The instincts of men are always right in this and all cognate matters. All formalism is offensive to good taste. The painter does not study landscape in a garden. Formal isles, closely-trimmed trees, rose bushes on the top of tall sticks, flowers tied to supports, vines trained upon trellises, lakes with clipped and pebbled margins and India-rubber swans—these are not picturesque. There is no more inspiration in them than there would be in a row of tenement houses in the city. The painter looks for beauty out where nature reigns undisturbed amid her imperfections,—where the aisles are made by the deer going to his lick; where the trees are never trimmed save by the lightning or the hurricane; where the rose-bushes spread their branches and the vines trail themselves at liberty; and where the lake looks up into the faces of trees centuries old, and hems itself in with thickets of alders and green reaches of flags and rushes, and throbs to the touch of the mountain breeze, while on its bosom

> "The black duck, with her glossy breast
> Sits swinging silently."

A little child whose head is piled with laces and ribbons, whose dress is a mass of embroidery, and who is booted and gloved and otherwise oppressed by parental vanity and extravagance, is not picturesque, any further than its face goes. The portrait painter will cling to the face and let the clothes alone. All this trickery of art, brought into comparison or contrast with the simple beauty of nature, is offensive. Yet a little beggar boy, with an old straw hat on, and with bare, brown feet, and a burnt shoulder which his torn shirt refuses to cover, would be a painter's joy. Here would be drapery that he would delight to paint, simply because there would be no formality about it. It is impossible for us to know how ridiculous a dress-coat is until we see it in a statue. We are obliged to put all our modern sages and heroes into togas and blankets and long cloaks in order to make them presentable to posterity.

We never find groups of accordant, striking facts like these—and their number could be largely increased—without finding that they are all strung together by an important law. All life demands room and freedom—

freedom to manifest itself in every way, according to the law of its being and the range of its circumstances. All life is individual and characteristic, and comes reluctantly under the sway of outside forces. It is not natural to be proper, or to love propriety. In saying this I simply mean that it is against nature to bring one's individuality under the curbing and controlling hands of others—to make the notions of the world the law and limit of one's liberty, and to square every word and every act by arbitrary rules imposed by cliques and customs. A man who has been clipped in all his puttings-forth, and modelled by outside hands and outside influences, until it is apparent that he is governed from without rather than from within, is just as unnatural an object as a tree that has been clipped and tied and bent until its top has grown into the form of a cube. Thus the reason why Miss Nancy is not popular, and why the women refuse to delight in him, is, that he is not his own master—that he has, in himself, no independent life. It is not proper that he give utterance to his impulses;—so he suppresses them. It is not proper that he frankly reveal the emotions of his heart; so he conceals them. It is not proper that he enter enthusiastically into any work or any pleasure; so he is a constant check to the enthusiasm of others. It is not proper that he speak the words that spring to his lips when his weak sensibilities are touched; so he studies his language, and shapes his phrases to the accepted models. Thus is he shortened in on every side, until his individuality is all gone, and the humanity in him becomes as characterless as its expression. Every utterance of his life is made with a well-measured reference to certain standards to which he is an acknowledged slave.

A scrupulously proper man is often a self-deceiver, and not unfrequently an intentional deceiver of others. I do not say that he is necessarily a scoundrel or a fool. He may be very little of either, and he may be a little of both. These two words, which sound rather roughly, will give us, I think, a faithful index to his character. A man who is punctiliously proper has usually become so in consequence of an attempt to cover up his mental deficiencies or his moral obliquities. Punctilious propriety is always pretentious, and pretentiousness is always an attempt at fraud. A shallow mind is very apt to clothe itself with propriety as with a garment. A brain that cannot handle large things very often undertakes to manage a multiplicity of little things, and runs naturally into those minute proprieties of life which are showy, and which appear to the ignorant to indicate great powers and acquisitions in reserve. Most proper men are nothing but a shell, although many of them pass with the world for more. Their life is all on the outside, and is placed and kept there for show.

We approach them, and very frequently find them so well guarded that we do not get a look into their emptiness for a long time. We examine them as we would a hillside strewn with fragments and planted with boulders of marble. We are obliged to dig to learn whether the signs we see are from an out-cropping ledge, or an outside deposition. Sometimes the plunge of a single question will reveal the whole story. A man with large brains and a large life in him has something to do besides attending to the notions of other people. He has at least no motive to deceive the world by striving to appear to be more than he is.

I have said that there are some men who are punctiliously proper for the purpose of covering their moral obliquities. The virtue of a prude is always to be suspected. "So you have been looking after the bad words," was savage old Dr. Johnson's reply to the very proper woman who found fault with him for introducing so many indecent words into his dictionary. There are few men who have not frequently, during their lives, broken their way through a crust of punctilious propriety into hearts full of all the blackness of sensuality and sin. The world is full of hypocrisy, and hypocrisy is nothing more than appearing to be what one is not. Indeed, I believe that one of the strongest motives operative in the world to render men scrupulously proper in their deportment and behavior is sin.

I make no hesitation in saying that shallowness and sensuality are the leading ingredients in the majority of the exceedingly proper characters with which I am acquainted.

Leaving this particular phase of my subject, I wish to call attention to the well-recognized fact that all perfect people are bores. A perfect character in a novel has no more power over a reader—no more foothold among his sympathies—than a proposition in mathematics would have. Of all stupid creations that the brain of man has given birth to, there are none so stupid as the perfect men and women whom we find upon the pages of fiction. Sometimes we find in actual life a character so symmetrical, so rounded off at the corners, and smoothed at the edges, and polished on the sides, and unexceptionable in all its manifestations, that we cannot find fault with it; yet we find it impossible for us to love it. Such a character gets beyond the reach of our sympathies. Human affection is like ivy. It cannot cling to glass; it must plant its feet in imperfections. It is not to be denied that imperfection is the true flavor of humanity. The mind refuses to sympathize where it does not exist. What the world would call a perfect man—what would be adjudged a perfect man by the best standards—would be as tasteless as a last year's apple. A perfect woman could no more be loved than she could be hated. I never saw a man with a perfect face—a face modelled so symmetrically and so perfectly that no fault could be found with it—who was not more or less a numskull. A pretty man is always a pretty fool; and the more symmetrical the features of a woman are, the more does she approach to the style of beauty and expression and native gifts of a porcelain doll. The mind and the character can be so symmetrical that they will lose all charm and all significance. They descend into simple prettiness, which is simple insipidity.

I say that imperfection is the true flavor of humanity. In explanation, I ought to say that all individuality is either based upon it or pre-supposes it. For instance: the preponderance of certain powers and qualities of mind and character in me, over certain other powers and qualities, and the weakness and imperfection of these latter as related to the former, and to the individualities of others, make my individuality what it is. If in me all mental and moral powers were in equipoise—if I were a symmetrical man, as the first Adam may possibly have been—I should have no individuality, no qualities that would distinguish me—no weaknesses that would furnish footholds for human sympathy—no freshness and flavor. A whole world full of perfect men and women, each one like every other, would be unutterably stupid. Where there is no weakness there is no individuality; where there is no individuality there is no true humanity; where there is no true humanity there is no sympathy; and where there is no sympathy there is no pleasure. We demand that a man shall live according to his law—develop himself according to his law—manifest and express himself according to his law; and then he will become the object of our sympathy or antipathy, according to our law. We demand that the true flavor of every individuality shall be declared, and not be masked by the imposition of conventional regulations.

If every tree in the world were perfect, according to any recognized standard, then all the trees would be alike, and would cease to be attractive and picturesque. We keep all perfect things out of pictures, because they are formal and tasteless. A bran new cottage, with a picket fence around it, and every thing cleaned up about it, is too perfect to be picturesque. An old, tumble-down mill, with rude and rotten timbers, and a wheel outside, is decidedly picturesque, because its imperfections make it informal. The most unattractive of all houses is a model house. A house that no man can find fault with, is a house that no man can love. It is precisely thus with human character and with men. A proper, perfect, "model" man, is an unlovable man. A sphere cannot be made to fit an angle, and a spherical character has no point of sympathy with one that is thrown into the angles necessary for individuality. So we neither love symmetry and perfection in men, according to any recognized standard, nor the appearance of them. We demand not only that men shall have individuality, but that they shall express it in their language and their lives. In society we demand variety; and in order to have it, men must act out themselves. The harmony and sweetness of social life consist in the adjustment of the strong points of some to the weak points of others.

With these facts so very evident as they must be to all thoughtful minds, it is strange that such an effort is made to bring all men to a certain standard and style of life. I do not believe there is a country on the face of the earth where public opinion and fashion and conventional and individual notions, exercise so despotic a sway as they do in America. There is, in this "free country," no play to individuality tolerated. No room is made for the peculiarities of a man—no freedom is given to his mode of manifestation. A man who has peculiar manners, and whose style of individuality is marked, has no room allowed to him at all. He is very likely to be called a fool, and laughed at by his inferiors. We take no pains to look through the outside to find the heart and soul, and refuse to see excellence behind manifestations that offend our notions or our tastes. We go to hear a preacher, and if he do not happen to have the externals, and the style of delivery which we most admire, we condemn him at once. We make no room for his individuality, and allow to it no freedom of manifestation. Room and freedom—that which the ocean has, that which the rivers have, that which the forest has, and that from which all of them derive their beauty and their glory —room and freedom are denied to men by men who need both, quite as much as their fellows.

The choicest food of the gossips is the personal peculiarities of their acquaintances. The grand staple of ridicule is this same individuality, whose importance I have endeavored to illustrate. All the small wits of society busy themselves upon the eccentricities of those around them. Church and creed, party and platform, fashion and custom, all direct themselves against the development of individuality. Sensitive natures shrink before such an array of influences, and retire into themselves, drawing back and keeping in check all their out-reaching individuality. Many a man, indeed, who would face a cannon's mouth without trembling, flinches when beset by ridicule. It is not the fault of society that the whole race of mankind are not reduced to a dead level of character, and a tasteless uniformity of life. Were it not that God does His work so strongly, it would have been undone long ago. As it is, we always have a few men and women who are true enough to God and themselves to keep the world from stagnation, and give zest to life. They sometimes shock Miss Nancy, but as they do not happen to care what Miss Nancy thinks of them, they manage to live and do something to keep Miss Nancy's friends from settling into chronic inanity.

LESSON XXII.

THE POETIC TEST.

> "I walked on, musing with myself
> On life and art, and whether, after all,
> A larger metaphysics might not help
> Our physics—a completer poetry
> Adjust our daily life and vulgar wants
> More fully than the special outside plans,
> Phalansteries, material institutes,
> The civil conscriptions and lay monasteries,
> Preferred by modern thinkers."
>
> MRS. BROWNING.

THE highest poetry is the purest truth. To learn whether any thing is as it ought to be, we have only to learn whether it is truly poetical. It is a popular fallacy to suppose that poetical things are necessarily fanciful, or imaginative, or sentimental—in other words, that poetry resides in that which is both baseless and valueless. In the popular thought, poetry is shut out of the realm of truth and reality.

The reason, I suppose, is, that poetry demands more of truth and harmony and beauty than is commonly found in the actualities of human life.

Let us suppose that in a country journey we arrive at the summit of a hill, at whose foot lies a charming village imbosomed in trees from the midst of which rises the white spire of the village church. If we are in a poetical mood, we say: "How beautiful is this retirement! This quiet retreat, away from the world's distractions and great temptations, must be the abode of domestic and social virtue—the home of contentment, of peace, and of an unquestioning Christian faith. Fortunate are they whose lot it is to be born and to pass their days here, and to be buried at last in the little graveyard behind the church." As we see the children playing upon the grass, and the tidy matrons sitting in their doorways, and the farmers at work in the fields, and the quiet inn, with its brooding piazzas like wings waiting for the shelter of its guests, the scene fills us with a rare poetic delight. In the midst of our little rapture, however, a communicative villager comes along, and we question him. We are shocked to learn that the inn is a very bad place, with a drunken landlord, that there is a quarrel in the church which is about to drive the old pastor away, that there is not a man in the village who would not leave it if he could sell his property, that the women give a free rein to their propensity for scandal, and that half of the children of the place are down with the measles.

The true poet sees things not always as they are, but as they ought to be. He insists upon congruity and consistency. Such a life should be in such a spot, under such circumstances; and no unwarped and unpolluted mind can fail to see that the poet's ideal is the embodiment of God's will. The poet's Indian is very different frem the real native American who has been exposed to the corrupting influences of the white man's civilization. The poet insists on seeing in the American Indian a noble manhood, simple tastes, freedom from all conventionality, heroic fortitude, and all those romantic qualities which a free forest life seems so well calculated to engender. He looks upon the deep, mysterious woods, traversed by nameless streams; the majestic mountains, haunted by shadows; the broad lakes, swept only by the wind and the wild man's oar, and he says: "it is fitting, and only fitting, that out of such a realm should come such a life." Which is the better and the more truthful Indian—that of the poet, or he who drank the rum of our fathers and then scalped them? The poet's village is the model village, and the poet's Indian is the model Indian. Both are built of the best and truest materials that God furnishes, and we see that when the actual village and the real Indian are tried by the poetic standard, they are tried by the severest standard that can be applied to them. The poet's ideal embodies God's ideal of a village and an Indian.

The grand, basilar idea of American institutions is human equality—the idea embodied in the American Declaration of Independence, that men are created free and equal, each with an independent, and all with a co-ordinate, right to life, liberty, and the pursuit of happiness. There is in this idea the highest poetry, because it is the transcendent truth; and there is no true poetry this side of the highest truth. Poetry follows the universal law, and is dependent for its quality upon its materials. In the degree in which its materials are fictitious and artificial, is it poor and false. The Pilgrim's Progress is essentially better poetry than the Paradise Lost, because it contains more of the truth as it is in the divine life of man.

The poetic test, then, is practically a very valuable one, in all the important matters that relate to our life. Much of that which is miscalled poetry has been based upon arbitrary and artificial distinctions in human society and human lot. The poet has often sung of thrones and palaces, of kings and queens, of men and women of gentle blood, of barons and knights and squires, of retainers and dependents, of patricians and plebeians, and thus drawn his grand interest from distinctions in which God and Nature have had no hand. There may be romance, fancy, imagination, sentiment, and even instruction in such compositions as these, but there is no poetry. They have not in them the immortal life and the motive power of truth. We have only to carry distinctions thus attempted to be glorified to their logical results to land in the slavery of the masses to the over-mastering few. Now there never was, and there never can be, any poetry in slavery. Since time began no true poet has undertaken to write a line in praise of slavery. Poets have always been, and they must necessarily forever be, the prophets and priests of freedom. Multitudes of men have undertaken to justify slavery by the Bible, by expediency, by history, by necessity, by philosophy, by the constitution of the country; but no man ever undertook to justify it by poetry. The most brilliant prize offered by a national committee for the best poem in praise of human slavery, would not be able to draw forth a single stanza from any man capable of writing a line of true poetry. Philosophical defences of slavery can be purchased, political justifications can be had at the small price of a small office, and Christian apologies to order, but, thank God! not one line in praise of slavery could be written by a true poet, if the wealth of the world were to be his reward.

We have in the present age a sickly, sentimental humanity which is busily endeavoring to pervert the sense and love of justice in mankind. It regards the disposition to do wrong as a disease, to be treated with appropriate emollients applied over the heart, or some gentle opiate or alterative taken through the ears. It pities the murderer, and aims to give the impression to him and to the world that he is a victim to the barbarous instincts of society in the degree by which his punishment is made severe. It aims to transform prisons into comfortable asylums, where those who have been so unfortunate as to burn somebody's house, or steal somebody's horse, or insert a dirk under somebody's waistcoat, may retire and repent of their little follies, and in the mean time get better food and lodging than they were ever able to steal. Punishment—retribution—these are words which make them shudder. Nothing in their view is proper but such treatment of the criminal, be it soft or severe, as will contribute to his reformation. The criminal has forfeited no rights, and society has no claims upon him, if he only repents; and all punishment inflicted beyond the measure necessary to secure repentance is cruel. We have a great deal of this; and more or less it is modifying theological systems and vitiating public policy. It is carried to such an extent, often, as to make of the greatest criminals notable martyrs. Society and the victim of wrong-doing are both forgotten in sympathy for the wrong-doer.

Now these sentimental sympathizers with criminals,

call themselves Christians, and are not willing to believe that any man can, in a truly Christian spirit, oppose their theories and their influence. They have been able to blind almost every sense in a man except the poetic sense; but to this they appeal in vain. "Poetic justice" maintains its purity. The reader of a novel, no matter how good or how bad he may be, demands that the villain of the book shall be punished as a matter of justice alike to him and to those who have been his victims. Nothing but justice—nothing but a fitting retribution—will satisfy. The poetic instinct demands a perfect system of rewards and punishments, and is as little satisfied when a hero succeeds indifferently, as when a scoundrel fails to be punished according to his deserts. There is no poetic fitness without justice—retribution, pound for pound, and measure for measure. Set any audience that can be gathered to watching a play in which criminal and crafty art is made to meet and master a guileless spirit and pollute a spotless womanhood, and the sympathies of the vilest will follow the victim, and, in the end, demand the punishment of the victor. Nothing will seem to any audience so entirely out of place as kind and gentle treatment toward the artful brute, and nothing more outrageously unjust than the idea that repentance is the principal end of his punishment. The poetic instinct of fitness once thoroughly roused, as it is in a story, a poem, or a play, will be satisfied with nothing but full suffering for every sin. Now I would trust this poetic instinct of fitness further than I would all the sympathies of the humanitarians, all the sophistries of the philosophers, all the subtleties of the theologians, and all the milder virtues of Christianity itself. To me, it is as authoritative as a direct revelation from God, and is equivalent to it.

Again, nothing is more apparent in American character and American life than a growing lack of reverence. It begins in the family, and runs out through all the relations of society. The parent may be loved, but he is much less revered than in the olden time. Parental authority is cast off early, and age and gray hairs do not command that tender regard and that careful respect that they did in the times of the fathers. In politics, it is the habit to speak in light and disrespectful terms of those whose experience gives them the right to counsel and command. Young men talk flippantly of "fossils," and "old fogies," and wonder why men who have been buried once will not remain quietly in their graves. Of course, when such a spirit as this prevails, there can be no reverence for authority, no respect for place and position, and no genuine and hearty loyalty. We nickname our Presidents; and "old Buck" and "old Abe" are spoken of as familiarly as if they were a pair of old oxen we were in the habit of driving. Every man considers himself good enough for any place, and great enough to judge every other man. If a pastor does not happen to suit a parishioner, the parishioner has no feeling of reverence for him that would hinder him from telling him so to his face. Every man considers himself not only as good and as great as any other man, but a little better and a little greater. No being but God is revered, and He, I fear, not overmuch. What we call "Young America" is made up of about equal parts of irreverence, conceit, and that popular moral quality familiarly known as "brass."

It is the habit to applaud Young America—to magnify the superior wisdom and efficiency of young men, to treat old age familiarly, and to compel those of superior years to ignore the honors with which God has crowned them. "Every dog has his day," we say, and we are impatient of a man who declines to step into retirement the moment that his hair turns gray, to make room for some specimen of Young America with a snub nose and a smart shirt-collar. Now, however this irreverence may be justified—and it is not only justified but shamelessly gloried in—it is not poetical. Poetry cannot be woven of improprieties. A people bowing with reverence to those in authority, and regarding with profound respect high official station; a family of children clinging, even through a long manhood and womanhood, around the form of an aged parent with assiduous attentions and tender reverence; a community or a nation of young men looking to age for wisdom and for counsel; universal respect for years on the part of the young—these are, and must forever remain, poetical. Out of reverence can be woven the most beautiful pictures which the poet's brain can conceive; but Young America can no more excite poetic sentiment, or inspire poetic imaginations, than the sham Havana it smokes, or the mongrel horse it drives. There is no poetry in an irreverent character, or in an irreverent community. Irreverence in any form will not stand the poetic test.

Americans boast habitually of their country, and their boastings always assume the poetic form. The ballot-box that they talk about is the ballot-box that ought to be and not the ballot-box that is. One would think, to hear what is said of the ballot-box, that it literally shines with glory, so that every American freeman who marches up to it to deposit the paper embodiment of his will, glows like a God in its light, and grows godlike by his act. If we are to believe Mr. Whittier, the poor voter sings on election day:

"The proudest now is but my peer,
The highest not more high;
To-day, of all the weary year,
A king of men am I.

> To-day, alike are great and small,
> The nameless and the known;
> My palace is the people's hall,
> The ballot-box my throne!"

This is a very splendid sort of a ballot-box, and he is a very fine sort of an American who sings about it; but what are the facts? There are a good many chances that the box stands in a corner grocery, and that the poor voter is led up to deposit his priceless ballot so drunk that he cannot walk without help. Mr. Whittier would have us believe that the poor voter sings:

> "To-day shall simple manhood try
> The strength of gold and land;
> The wide world has not wealth to buy
> The power in my right hand."

The truth is that gold and land try the very "simple manhood" as a rule, and very much less than the wide world is sufficient to buy the power in a great multitude of poor voters' hands. The poet sees what the ballot-box may be, ought to be, and, in some rare instances, really is. He unerringly seizes upon the dignity and majesty of self-government, the equal rights and privileges of manhood, and the dissipation of all distinctions in the exercise of the political franchise among freemen. The great truth of human equality inspires him, and he uses the ideal and possible ballot-box to illustrate it, and thus furnishes the standard by which the real ballot-box is to be judged.

The poetical view of our American system of government is that all men have a voice in the government; that we choose our own rulers and make our own laws; that no man has a hereditary right to rule, and that men are selected for the service of the people, in the construction and the execution of the laws, because of their fitness for office. Outside of this view, the American system of government has no beauty and no foundation in truth and justice. If we undertake to argue with a monarchist, we never bring forward any other. It has in it the essential element of poetry, because it does justice to the nature and character of man, and describes a perfect political society. The poetical view of the American system of government, is, then, the highest view. It covers the sovereignty of the citizen, and the wisdom of the popular voice. Around this idea the poets have woven their noblest songs; but again we ask what are the facts? The people are led by the nose by politicians; and not one officer of the government in one hundred is chosen to his place because of his fitness for it. The people do not nominate those who shall rule them, or those who shall make laws for them. Those whom the politicians do not nominate for office, nominate themselves. The political machinery of America practically takes the choice of rulers and officers out of the hands of the people, and puts it into the hands of a set of self-appointed leaders, whose patriotism is partisanship, and whose principal aim is to serve themselves and their friends, and use the people for accomplishing their purposes. No greater fiction was ever conceived than the pleasant one that the people of America govern America. The people of America, except in certain political revolutions, have always been governed by a company of self-appointed and irresponsible men, whose principal work was to grind axes for themselves. The poetry of American politics is then the severest standard by which to judge the reality of American politics.

Religious freedom is another poetical idea in which the American glories. It is essentially a poetical thought that every man is free to worship God according to the dictates of his own conscience—that there is no Church to domineer over the State, and no State to domineer over the Church, that the Bible is free, and that each individual soul is responsible only to its Maker. This great and beautiful liberty stirs us when we think of it as music would stir us, breathed from heaven itself. It is grand, God-begotten, belonging in the eternal system of things, full of inspiration. This religious freedom we claim as Americans. Some of us enjoy it; but the number is not large. The freedom of the sect is not greatly circumscribed, but the freedom of the individual is hardly greater in America than it is in those countries where an established church lays its finger upon every man. I would as soon be the slave of the Pope or the Archbishop as the slave of a sect. I would as readily put my neck under the yoke of a national church as under the yoke of a sect. It does not mend the matter that the multitude are willing slaves, and it certainly mars the matter that the sects themselves do what they can, in too many instances, to circumscribe each the other's liberty. Sects are religiously and socially proscribed by sects. Take any town in America that contains half a dozen churches, representing the same number of religious denominations, and it will be found that, with one, and that probably the dominant sect, it will be all that a man's reputation and position are worth to belong to another sect. Perfect religious freedom in America there undoubtedly is; but it is the possession of only here and there an individual. Prevalent uncharitableness and bigotry are incompatible with the existence of religious liberty anywhere.

It is thus that the poetic instinct grasps at truth and beauty, and fitness and harmony, wherever it sees it, and it is thus that it furnishes us (subordinate only to special, divine revelation) with the most delicate tests of human institutions, customs, and actions. Litmus-paper does not more faithfully detect the presence of an acid than the poetic instinct detects the false and foul in all that makes up human life. All that is grand

and good, all that is heroic and unselfish, all that is pure and true, all that is firm and strong, all that is beautiful and harmonious, is essentially poetical, and the opposite of all these is at once rejected by the unsophisticated poetic instinct.

Verily the poets of the world are the prophets of humanity! They forever reach after and foresee the ultimate good. They are evermore building the paradise that is to be, painting the millennium that is to come, restoring the lost image of God in the human soul. When the world shall reach the poet's ideal, it will arrive at perfection; and much good will it do the world to measure itself by this ideal, and struggle to lift the real to its lofty level.

LESSON XXIII.

THE FOOD OF LIFE.

"To the soul time doth perfection give,
And adds fresh lustre to her beauty still;
And makes her in eternal youth to live
Like her which nectar to the Gods doth fill.
The more she lives, the more she feeds on truth;
The more she feeds, the strength doth more increase;
And what is strength, but an effect in youth
Which, if time nurse, how can it ever cease?"

SIR J. DAVIES.

A HORSE can live, and do a good deal of dull work, on hay; but spirit and speed require grain. There is no self-supplied, perennial fountain within the animal that enables him to expend more in the way of muscular power than he receives in the way of muscular stimulus and nourishment. Food, in its quality and amount, up to the limit of healthful digestion, is set over against, and exactly measures, under ordinary circumstances, the quality and amount of labor of which a horse is capable. So, a cow can live on straw and corn-stalks; but it would not be reasonable to suppose that she would give any considerable amount of milk upon so slender a diet. We do not expect rich milk, in large quantities, to be yielded by a cow that is not bountifully fed with the most nutricious food. The same fact attaches to land. We cannot get out of land more than there is in it; and having once exhausted it, we are obliged to put into it, in fertilizers, all we wish to take from it in the form of vegetable growths. Wherever there is an outgo, there must be an equal income, or exhaustion will be the inevitable consequence.

The principle which these familiar facts so forcibly illustrate is a very important one, in its connection with human life. We cannot get any more out of human life than we put into it. All civilization is an illustration of what can be accomplished by feeding the human mind. All barbaric and savage life is an illustration of mental and moral starvation. The differences among mankind are the results of differences in the nourishment upon which their minds are fed. Eunice Williams, who was taken captive by the savages of Canada a hundred and fifty years ago, was the daughter of a most godly minister, of the old Puritan stamp; but a very few years of savage feeding made her a savage. Her mind was cut off from all other varieties of nourishment, and could only tend to savage issues. She kept a knowledge of her history, and many years after her capture revisited her home, accompanied by her tawny husband; but no persuasions could call her from her savage life and companionship. The conversion of men from heathenism to Christianity and Christian civilization is accomplished by introducing new food into their moral and mental diet. "A change of pastures makes fat calves," we are told; and any one who has noticed the effect upon an active mind of its translation from one variety of social and moral influences to another, will recognize the truth of the proverb.

If a man will call up his acquaintances, one by one, and mentally measure the results of their lives, he will be astonished to see how small those results are. He will also see that they are, under ordinary circumstances, in the exact proportion to the amount, and in correspondence with the variety, of the food they take in. It is astonishing to see how little it takes to keep some people, and how very little such people become on their diet. A man who shuts himself away from all social life, and lays by his reading, and declines all food that addresses itself to his sensational and emotional nature, and refuses that bread of life which comes down from heaven, and feeds himself only with relation to the accomplishment of some petty work, will become as thin and scrawny, mentally and morally, as the body of a half-starved Hottentot. It is the one curse of rural life that it does not have a sufficiency and a sufficient variety of food. The same scenes, the same faces, the same limited range of books, the same dull friends, exhausted long ago—no new nourishment for powers cloyed with their never-varying food—these are what make rural life, as it is usually lived, unattractive and most unfruitful. The fruits—the issues—of this life cannot be greater than the food it gets, and the food is very scanty. It is not necessary that it should be so, and sometimes it is not so; but the rule of common rural life is insufficiency of mental food, and consequent poverty of manifestation.

The utilitarian habits of New England, originating in necessity, and far outliving the circumstances in which they had their birth, have tended more than any other cause to make New England character unlovable. The saving of half-pence to add to one's store, and the denial to one's self and children of that which will delight the famished senses, and stir the thin emotions, and enlarge the range of experience, is the direct way of arriving at meanness of life. There are those who will not allow their families to cultivate flowers, because flowers are not useful, and they involve a waste of time and land. They will not have an instrument of music in their houses, because music is not useful, and it involves an expenditure of money, and the throwing away of a great deal of time. They will not buy pictures, because pictures are not useful, and because they cost money; so that many a rich man's parlor is as bare of ornament as a tomb would be. They will not attend a lecture, because, though it might furnish them with mental food for a month, it would not bring their shillings back to them. They will not attend a concert, because a concert is not useful. They will not hire a minister who possesses fine gifts—gifts that would enrich them mentally, morally, and socially—because they cannot afford it. So they take up with ministerial dry nursing, and one another's dry experiences, as spiritual food, in order to save a few more dollars.

There are a few of the severer virtues that will live upon a diet of this kind. Endurance, industry, a negative purity, thrift, integrity—these can live, and do live, after a sort, on a plain and scanty diet, and these, as we know, abound in New England. But generosity, hospitality, charity, liberality—all those qualities that enrich the character, and all those virtues that enlarge it and give it fulness and beauty and attractiveness, are always wanting among the class that sacrifices every thing for use. More cannot be got out of any life than is put into it. Modern chemistry analyzes soils, and ascertains exactly what they need to make them produce bountifully of any kind of grains and fruits. Wheat cannot be grown on land that does not contain the constituents of wheat; and if it be desirable to grow wheat, those constituents must be added to the soil. If any mental soil does not produce those vital manifestations and results which characterize a large, rich, and attractive life, then the constituents of that life must be introduced as nutriment.

One of the common experiences in the world of authorship is the writing of a single successful book, and the failure of all that follow it from the same pen. The explanation is, that the first book is the result of a life of feeding, and those that follow it come from an exhausted mind. There are many writers who, as soon as they begin to write, stop feeding, and in a very short time write themselves out. The temptation of the writer is to seclusion. His labors in a measure unfit him for social life, and for mingling in the every-day affairs of men. He is apt to become warped in his sentiments, and morbid in his feelings, and to grow small and weak as his works increase. The greatest possible blessing to an author is compulsory contact with the world—every-day necessity to meet and mingle with men and women—social responsibilities and business cares, and the consequent necessity of keeping up with the events and the literature of his time. An author in this position not only keeps a healthy mind, but he takes in food every day which his individuality assimilates to itself, and utters as the expression of its life. I have no belief that Shakspeare would ever have given us his immortal plays, but for the necessities which brought him so much into contact with men. Outside of his authorship, he lived an active, practical life—trod the boards of a theatre, managed men, looked after his money, rubbed against society in multiplied ways—and kept himself strong, healthy, and abundantly fed with that food which was necessary to him.

Shakspeare had genius, it is true, but genius without food is quite as helpless as a barren acre. All great geniuses are immense feeders. All true and healthy geniuses fasten for food upon every thing and every body. Their antennæ are always out for the apprehension of ideas, and their mouths always open for their reception. Walter Scott was engaged in the active duties of the legal profession when writing his novels, and there was not a legend of Scotland, nor a bit of history or gossip, nor an old story-teller that lived within fifty miles of him, that he did not lay under tribute for mental food. It is declared, to the everlasting disgrace of Goethe, that he practiced upon the affections of women, even to old age, that he might gather food for poetry. Byron traversed Europe in search of adventure, and rummaged the scenes of legend and story for food for his voracious senses and sensibilities. His Childe Harold is nothing but the record of his tireless foraging. All men who have produced much have fed bountifully.

The writers are few in whom we do not notice something painfully wanting. We do not always understand what it is, but we know that, while we may accord to them good sense, and even genius, they fail to satisfy us. There is some good thing which they lack—something unbalanced and partial and one-sided about them. We presume that this is often the result of a constitutional defect, but in most instances it is attributable to insufficient nourishment in some department of their nature. "All but," is the appropriate epitaph for the tombstone of many an author; and if we look carefully into his history we shall find an answer to the question: "All but what?" We shall find, perhaps, that he is a recluse, that his social nature is not fed at all, and that he is, of course, unsympathetic. This is a very frequent cause of dissatisfaction with an author, as it always gives a morbid tinge to his writings. Dickens is eminently a social man, and eminently healthy and sympathetic. Possibly an author may starve his senses and become purely reflective, yielding up his points of contact with the outside world, and shutting the channels by which the qualities of things find their way to his mind. Not unfrequently a man's domestic affections may be starved, or ill fed, and if so, the fact is sure to be betrayed in his writings. And if a writer's religious nature be starved, it invariably vitiates all his characteristic works. No man who shuts out God and heaven from his life can write without betraying the poverty of his diet. If an author would write satisfactorily, touching all kinds of human nature and all sides of human nature, he must feed every department of his own nature, for he has nothing to give that he does not receive.

As in animal, so in mental life, there are gormandizing and gluttony, tending always to paralysis of voluntary effort. The devouring of facts, as they are found both in nature and in books, indulgence in social pleasures immoderately and constantly, pietism that feeds exclusively upon the things of religion, the feasting of the imagination upon the creations of fiction—all these are debilitating; and a blessed thing to the world is it that they unfit the mind for writing at all, as the overfeeding of the body unfits its organs for labor. Plethoric minds do not trouble the world with books, or with conversation, or with preaching. Activity simply demands food enough, and in sufficient variety, to feed its powers while operative, from day to day. This is the reason why immensely learned men have rarely done much for the world. Many of them have won reputations, like remarkably fat steers, for breadth of back and depth of brisket, but they are never known to move more than their own enormous bulks. Beyond a certain point of mental feeding, over and above the necessities of labor, the mind gets sleepy and clumsy.

I have alluded to authors, particularly, because, unlike the world in general, they give form and record to their life. The masses of men live as authors live, but their lives are not put down in books, so that the public may read and measure them. We will suppose that two men are fed upon the same diet. Each shall have sufficient food for his religious, social, esthetic, domestic, sensational, and emotional natures, yet only one of them shall embody in books the life which he draws from these varieties of nourishment. The other lives essentially the same life, but it fails of record. It may be as rich and characteristic, in every particular, as that of the author, but it fails of artistic form because, perhaps, he lacks the peculiar mental gift required for its construction. So the real life of the author and the life of his reader may be the same, the one having advantage over the other in no particular, and the fact that one is embodied in artistic forms conferring upon it no essential excellence. What I have said about authors, therefore, applies to all mankind, engaged in whatever calling or profession. If any portion of any man's nature be not well fed, he will betray the fact in his life. Poverty of food in any particular will surely bring poverty of manifestation in that department of life which is deprived of its natural nourishment.

A familiar illustration of the failure of a life to secure its appropriate food, will be found in men and women who live unmarried. An old bachelor will sooner or later betray the fact that his finer affections are starved. It is next to impossible for him to hide from the world the wrong to which he is subjecting himself. His character will invariably show that it is warped and weak and lame, and his life will be barren of all those manifestations which flow from domestic affections abundantly fed. Here and there, one like Washington Irving will nourish a love transplanted to Heaven, and bring around him the sweet faces and delicate natures of women, to minister to a thirsting heart, and preserve, as he did, his geniality and tenderness to the last; but such as he are comparatively few. An old bachelor, voluntarily single, always betrays a nature badly fed in one of its important departments. So, too, those who marry, but who are not blest with children, betray the lack of food. Many of these hunger through life for children to feed their affections, and take on peculiarities that betray the fact that something is wrong with them. Some adopt children in order to supply a want which seems imperative, and others take pets of different kinds to their bosoms, ranging through the scale from birds to bull-dogs. It is a familiar trick of starved faculties and affections to take on a morbid appetite, and feed themselves on the strangest of supplies.

So, if a man would live a full and generous life, he must supply it with a full and generous diet. So far as his ability will go, he should make his home the embodiment of his best taste. There should be abundant meaning in its architecture. There should be pictures upon its walls, and books upon its shelves and tables. All the domestic and social affections should be abundantly fed there. His table should be a gathering place for friends. Music should minister to him. He should bring himself into contact with the great and wise and good, who have embalmed their lives in the varied forms of art. The facts that live in the earth under his feet, the beauty that spreads itself around him, and all those truths which appeal to his religious nature, are food which should minister to his life. An irreligious man—no matter what his genius may be—is always a starveling. An unsocial man can by no possibility lead a true life. A man's nature should be thrown wide open at every point, to drink in the nourishment that comes from the healthy sources of supply; and thus only may his life become abundantly rich and beautiful. I repeat the proposition that I started with: we cannot get more out of human life than we put into it.

There is another aspect of this subject that I have barely space to allude to. The illustration with which this article opens, touching the effects of hay and grain respectively upon the life of the horse, suggests that the food with which our bodies are nourished may have an important bearing upon our mental and moral life. Of this I have no doubt. Coarse food, made of material but feebly vitalized, makes coarse men and women. Muscular tissues not formed from choice material, brains built of poor stuff, nervous fibres to which the finest and most delicate food has not ministered, are not the instruments of the highest grade of mental life. The dispensation of sawdust is passed away. It is pretty well understood that the most complicated, the noblest, and the finest creature in the world requires the best food the world can produce; and that he requires it in great variety. If a man leads simply an animal life—eating, working, and sleeping—let him feed as animals do; but if he lives a life above animals, as a social and religious being, then let him take food that gives pleasure to his palate, and pluck and power to all the instruments of his mind. Hay may answer very well for a mind that moves at the rate of only three miles an hour; but a mile was never yet made "inside of 2:40" without grain.

LESSON XXIV.

HALF-FINISHED WORK.

"Ah God! well, art is long!
And life is short and fleeting.
What headaches have I felt and what heart-beating,
When critical desire was strong.
How hard it is the ways and means to master
By which one gains each fountain head!
And ere one yet has half the journey sped
The poor fool dies—O sad disaster!"

BROOKS' TRANSLATION OF FAUST.

MANKIND are "nothing, if not critical;" and nothing would seem to be criticism with them but fault-finding. It is astonishing to see what a number of architects there are in the world—how many people there are who feel competent to give an opinion upon buildings in course of erection on the public streets. If a dwelling is going up, there is not a day of its progress in which its builder or architect is not convicted of being a fool, by any number of wise people who judge him on the evidence of a half-finished structure. When the dwelling is completed, it usually "looks better than they ever supposed it could;" but they learn nothing from this, though the proverb that "only fools criticize half-finished work" is a good deal older than they are. Every man who builds is obliged to take this running fire of fault-finding. Passing a new church recently, in the company of an architect, I asked him what he thought of the building. "I can tell better when the staging is down," was his reply. He knew enough not to criticize half-finished work, while probably a hundred men, knowing nothing of architecture whatever, had, during that very day, freely given their opinion of the building in the most unqualified way.

Did it ever occur to the reader of this essay that nearly all the judgments that are made up and expressed in this world relate to half-finished work? We hear a great deal of criticism indulged in with regard to American society. I have no doubt that this criticism is just, in a certain sense, but American society is only a half-finished structure. If it had arrived at the end of improvement and growth; if the elements which enter into it had already organized themselves in their highest form; if the creation of a high, refined, and beautiful society were not a thing of time; if such a society did not depend upon the operation of forces that require a great range of influences and circumstances, then the criticism might be entirely just; but it is as unreasonable to expect a high grade of social life in America, at this point of American history, as it is to expect perfection in a church before the carpenters get out of it, and the staging is down. Wealth, learning, culture, leisure—these cannot be so combined in this country yet as to give us the highest grade and style of social life. We are all at work upon the structure, and unless American ideas are incurably bad, and we are faithless to our duties, American society will be good when the work upon it is completed. No society is to be condemned so long as it is progressive toward a goodly completeness.

Men and women are always judging one another before they are finished. A raw boy, with only the undeveloped elements of manhood in him, is denounced as a dunce. A light-hearted, sportive girl, with an incontinent overflow of spirits, is condemned as a hoiden. Neither boy nor girl is half made. There is only the frame-work of the man and woman up, and it does not appear what they are to become. A young man is wild, and judged accordingly. It is not remembered that there are various modifying influences to be brought to bear upon him, before he will be a man. We see the bold outline of a new house, and we say that it is not beautiful. Soon, however, a piazza is built here, and a dormer is pushed out there, and gracefully modelled chimneys pierce the roof, and cornice and verandah and tower are added, until the structure stands before us complete in beauty, convenience, and strength. When we condemn a young man we do not stop to think that he is not done,—that there is a wife to place upon one side of him, and children to be grouped upon the other, and sundry relations to be adjusted before we can tell any thing about him at all.

There is nothing more common in experience and observation than the partiality felt by young and unmarried men for the society of married women, and the love of unmarried young women for the society of married men. I suppose that nearly every young man and young woman has a time of feeling that all the desirable matches in the world are disposed of, and that the marriageable young persons left are really very insipid companions. This is entirely natural, but exceedingly unreasonable. To expect a man to be as much of a man without a wife as with one, is just as reasonable as to expect a half-finished house to be as beautiful as a finished one. It is impossible for an unmarried man, other things being equal, to be as agreeable a companion as a married man; and lest I be suspected of a jest in this statement, I wish to assure my reader that I am entirely in earnest. Intimate contact with the nature of a good woman, in the relation of marriage, is just as necessary to the completeness of manhood, as the details of an architectural design are to the homely conveniences around which they are made to cluster. Every man is a better man for having children, and the more he extends those relations which grow out of the family life, the more does he open up to culture and carry to completeness the very choicest portions of his manly nature. It is natural, therefore, that the unmarried woman should become possessed of the notion that all the desirable men are married, and that the unmarried man should be the subject of a similar mistake with relation to the other sex. It must be remembered that men and women are made desirable by matrimony, and that half-finished work should not be subjected to any sweeping judgments.

Men and women are always turning out differently from what we expected and predicted they would. Men who have been laughed at and slighted during all their early life, become, quite to our surprise, very important and notable persons, and we are mortified to ascertain that we have been criticizing half-finished men. The college faculty give a diploma to some very slow young man, with great reluctance, but in the course of twenty years he completes himself, and when he comes back to honor them with a visit they make very low bows to him. All young people are pieces of unfinished work, to be judged very carefully, and always to be regarded as incomplete. We can say that we do not like their general style, as we would say that we do not like the style of an unfinished house. Grecian may not be to our liking, and we may prefer Gothic.

It seems to me that the Christian Church suffers more from the judgments of those who criticize unfinished work than any organized body of men and women. Here is an organization whose members do not pretend to perfection; whose whole theory forbids any such idea. They are disciples—learners of the Divine Master. They are members of a school in which none ever arrives at fulness of knowledge. Their prayer is that they may grow; and they know that if they have the true life in them they will grow while they live. If there is one thing in the world of which they are painfully conscious, it is that they are pieces of unfinished work. Some of the members are very much lower in the scale of completeness than others. In some there is only a confused pile of timber and bricks. In others only a part of the frame is up, or the walls are hardly more than begun. In others, perhaps, the roof is on. In comparatively few do we see the outlines all defined and the rooms in a good degree of completeness. In none of them is there a perfected structure, and none see and acknowledge their incompleteness more than those whose characters are farthest advanced toward perfection.

Now I put it to the world outside of the Christian Church to say if it has been entirely fair, and just in its judgments of the Church. Has it not judged Christianity by these imperfect disciples, and has it not condemned these imperfect disciples because they are not what they never pretended to be? Has it not criticized half-finished work, and condemned, not only the work, but Christianity itself, because this work was not up to the sample? It is very common to hear men say that such and such a Christian is no better than the average of people outside of the Christian Church, thus condemning the genuineness of his character because he is not a perfect Christian. A house is a house, even if it be only half-finished. At least, it is not any thing else; and as Christians cannot by any possibility be perfected on the instant, it follows that the large majority of Christians must be in various stages of progress—nay, that most of this large majority are not even half-finished. The Christian Church itself is a piece of unfinished work, and every individual member is the same. It is not pretended that either is any thing else. I never knew a Christian to set himself up as a pattern. So far as I know, they are very shy of pretension, and deprecate nothing more than the thought that anybody should take them for finished specimens of the work of Christianity in human life and character.

A sermon upon any important subject is always a piece of unfinished work. I once heard a famous preacher say that he could preach throughout his whole life on the text, "the heart is deceitful above all things and desperately wicked," and even then have something left to say. The statement illustrates the many-sidedness of truth, and the multitude of its relations to the life of the individual and the world. Any sensible preacher knows that, within the compass of a single sermon, he can only present a single aspect of a great and important truth, yet he is criticized as if it had been expected that the work of a dozen volumes could be crowded into the utterances of half an hour. What is called an "exhaustive" sermon would exhaust an audience long before it would its subject. A sermon is only the dab of a brush upon a great picture, and if it gives a single striking view of a single great truth, it accomplishes its object. It must necessarily be an unfinished piece as regards its exposition of truth; and the same may be said of any essay on any subject. Every writer begins in the middle of things, and leaves off in the middle ot things; and every thing he writes relates at some point to every thing that everybody has written. No man cleans up the field over which he walks, and leaves nothing to be said; and the best we do is unfinished work.

There are those who, in view of the sin and suffering which appear on every hand, are moved to impugn the goodness and love of Him who created the world by His power, and sustains and orders it by His providence. Millions are whelmed in the darkness of heathenism; other millions are bound by the chains of slavery; the oppressor is clothed in purple and fine linen; the beautiful and innocent are the victims of treacherous lust; children cry for bread beneath the windows of luxury; justice is denied to the poor by men who take bribes of wealth; and deceit circumvents and baffles honor. Such a world as this the critics condemn as a failure, which reflects alike upon the benevolence and power of its Maker; but these men have an eminent place among the fools who criticize half-finished work. If they could have witnessed the creation of the earth, and watched it through all the processes by which it was prepared for the reception of the human race, they would doubtless have been quite as critical as they are now, and quite as unreasonable. Suppose a man should visit his pear-trees in midsummer, and on tasting the fruit upon them, should condemn them and order them to be cut down and removed—how should we characterize his folly? He has criticized half-finished fruit, and made a fatal mistake. It is just as unreasonable to condemn a half-finished world as a half-finished pear. Human society must be brought to perfection by regularly instituted and slowly operating processes. It may take as long to perfect society as it did to create the world that it lives on; and God is not to be found fault with for the flavor of a fruit slowly ripening beneath the light of His smile and the warmth of His love, but not yet fully ripe.

Mr. Buckle has undertaken to write a history of civilization, or, rather, he has commenced to write an introduction to a history of civilization. His progress has not been great, and he doubtless realizes that he has undertaken a task which he can never finish. He will probably labor upon it while he lives, and then some other daring man will take up the thread where he will drop it, and go on until he in turn will be obliged to relinquish his unfinished task to a successor. When the work shall be finished, after its original design, it will doubtless be found to be antiquated. It undertook to organize a half-finished life—to reason upon forces that had only half revealed their nature and their power—to develop principles whose relations were imperfectly known. In short, it must necessarily prove to be a half-finished history of a half-finished civilization, whose every newly-opened event will throw a modifying light on all that shall have preceded it.

We have, therefore, but little finished work in this

world. Not a finished character lives among mankind. No nation of the world illustrates a consummate civilization. All presentations of truth, of whatever nature and relation, are necessarily incomplete. Life is too short, comprehension too limited in its grasp, and expression too feeble or too clumsy, to allow the mind fully to organize, vitalize, and fill out to roundness and just proportion, a single creature of legitimate art. It is, therefore, literally true that the criticisms of the world are the judgments of the world's half-finished men on the world's half-finished affairs. Imperfection sits in judgment on incompleteness, and the natural consequence is that criticism, in whatever field of demonstration, is little more than a record of notions which assume to array themselves against other notions, which may be better or worse than those that oppose them.

It is with a depressing sense of the incompleteness of these lessons in life, that I now indite their closing paragraph. I cannot but be aware that the criticisms I have indulged in relate very largely to half-finished work, and I painfully feel that they are the product of a most imperfect judgment. If the reader has found them kind, charitable, hopeful—tending toward that which is good—and lenient toward human frailty, loyal to common sense, and faithful to virtue; if he has found in them that which leaves him a larger and a more liberal man—advanced in some degree toward that perfection which we are ever striving for, but which we never reach, then my aim has been accomplished, and I bid him God speed!

THE END.

www.ingramcontent.com/pod-product-compliance
Lightning Source LLC
LaVergne TN
LVHW010202110826
845151LV00002B/586

* 9 7 8 1 4 2 5 5 3 5 3 8 4 *